Ten Plays of Terror

Ten Plays of Terror

Dramatic Adaptations for Amateur Players

Clay Franklin

Foreword by Anne Baxter

South Brunswick and New York: A. S. Barnes and Company
London: Thomas Yoseloff Ltd

A. S. Barnes and Co., Inc.
Cranbury, New Jersey 08512

Thomas Yoseloff Ltd
Magdalen House
136-148 Tooley Street
London SE1 2TT, England

Library of Congress Cataloging in Publication Data

Franklin, Clay.
    Ten plays of terror.

    CONTENTS: Lament for Juliet. — The tell-tale heart. — The cradle will rock. — Nobody's house. [etc.]
    1. Amateur theatricals.   2. Stage adaptations.
I. Title.
PN6120.A5F555   812'.5'2   78-75349
ISBN 0-498-02325-7

PRINTED IN THE UNITED STATES OF AMERICA

Contents

Foreword

This collection of short dramas fills a crying need. Television has usurped creative play for too many young people. It's heartening to know *Ten Plays of Terror* is available as an intriguing collection of launching pads. They are refreshingly literary and cleverly attention-getting.

—Anne Baxter

Acknowledgments

Grateful acknowledgment is made to the following publishers:

Dodd, Mead and Company, for "The Canterville Ghost" by Oscar Wilde, in *The Ghost Story Omnibus*.

Harcourt, Brace, Jovanovich, Inc., for "Nobody's House" by A. M. Burrage, in *Omnibus of Crime*.

The Hamlyn Publishing Group, and A. P. Watt Ltd., for "The Decoy" by Algernon Blackwood, in *Tales of the Uncanny*.

Little, Brown and Company, for "The Cradle Will Rock" by Harriet Beecher Stowe, in *The Pearl of Orr's Island*.

Lothrop, Lee and Shepard, for "The Wind in the Rose-Bush" by Mary Wilkins Freeman, in *Ladies of Horror*.

The Williams and Wilkins Company, for "The Red Rag Under the Churn" by Alice Childs, in *A Treasury of Southern Folklore*.

Introduction

These play adaptations of well-known short stories were written for easy staging. The names of the authors are mentioned and gratefully acknowledged. Some of the plots have been expanded to add dramatic impact.

Pieces of scenery can be used but are not necessary, for various pieces of furniture can suggest the proper room. Instead of opening and closing actual doors, it can be done by pantomime. This calls for imagination on the part of actors and audience that can be a stimulating experience.

Instead of programs, the cast of characters and settings can be announced.

If lighting equipment is readily available, the proper illumination can add atmosphere to a particular scene. Spot lighting can also be effective.

To establish the mood, appropriate music can be played a minute or two before the play begins.

A page of Production Notes follows each play.

Even if a curtain is not used, that term is mentioned to denote the ending of each play.

May you enjoy creating a spooky time for your audience.

Ten Plays of Terror

Lament For Juliet

This is an adaptation of a short story that is entitled "The Spasm" in one volume and "Nerves" in another collection. It was written by Guy de Maupassant.

CAST OF CHARACTERS

NARRATOR — An articulate man or woman
MONSIEUR RENAULT — A distressed, middle-aged gentleman
JULIET RENAULT — A frail girl, age 18
PROSPER — A respectful valet

Scene — The sitting room in Monsieur Renault's apartment in Lorraine, Paris.

Time — A November evening a century ago.

Lament For Juliet

The sitting room in Monsieur Renault's apartment is suggested by a few pieces of furniture such as an easy chair at right center with a table beside it. Another chair is placed at left center. On the table is a tray with tea pot and cup, a candle in holder, and a handbell. A frame to represent a fireplace is placed down right. A few logs are beside it. Down left is an invisible doorway that leads to street.

The lighting is dim on the setting.

MONSIEUR RENAULT, JULIET *and* PROSPER *stand immovable at up center. Each of them is holding a death mask in front of face.*

NARRATOR *enters from down right and glances toward the figures.*

NARRATOR
(Cordially, to audience, indicating the three people)
As you will notice, the three people behind me do not appear alive at the moment. They have been dead for almost a century. That is why they are wearing death masks.
(He paces about a few steps)
Stories of the supernatural are still being written — but somehow they can't match with those of a bygone era. In a few moments these cadavers will come alive and present a story written by Guy de Maupassant in the nineteenth century.
(He takes a small envelope from his pocket)
In this envelope is some magic powder. I shall sprinkle this over them — and with luck and your concentration — the cast of players will become alive and introduce themselves.
(He dips fingers in envelope and throws some powder toward the three people. Then he crosses beside MONSIEUR RENAULT and snaps his fingers twice)

*(*MONSIEUR RENAULT *slowly lowers his mask. Then without moving his body or head he hands mask to NARRATOR)*

RENAULT
(With dignity)
I am Monsieur Renault. Because I am wealthy most people consider me a fortunate man. Alas, sorrow shares a large part of my life.

*(*NARRATOR *crosses to* JULIET *and snaps his fingers twice.* JULIET *lowers her mask and gives it to* NARRATOR*)*

JULIET
(Solemnly)
My name is Juliet Renault. Because all sorts of afflictions have been my constant companions, I never knew the love of a young man.

*(*NARRATOR *crosses to* PROSPER *and snaps his fingers twice.* PROSPER *lowers his mask and hands it to* NARRATOR.*)*

PROSPER
(Humbly)
Prosper is the name I answer to. And as valet to Monsieur Renault, I am frequently called to attend his every whim.

NARRATOR
(To audience)
And now by our magic power of imagination — we shall see the sitting room in Monsieur Renault's apartment located in Lorraine, France. So let us be quiet for a moment and expect the unusual to happen.

(The three figures remain motionless for another moment. Then RENAULT *crosses slowly to easy chair.* PROSPER *crosses to table.* JULIET *exits off left.* PROSPER *lights candle)*

(Lights come up on living room area)

(Sound of wind)

NARRATOR
(Pleased)
Thank you for concentrating. As you see, magic has happened. A few hours ago Monsieur Renault returned home after attending a sad event. *(He exits down right with death masks)*

PROSPER
(About to pour a cup of tea)
Do have a cup of tea, monsieur. It will soothe you.
RENAULT
(Declining with a wave of his hand as he paces about)
Alas, nothing I can drink will calm my grief. Even the wind
sounds mournful.
PROSPER
It does, sir. But try not to torment yourself.
RENAULT
My sorrow seems to linger on. Years ago it was a sad farewell to
my beloved wife. Today the grave has demanded my only
daughter.
PROSPER
You're trembling, sir. A cup of tea will warm you.
RENAULT
(Sits on easy chair)
Very well, Prosper. It may be a small comfort.

(PROSPER pours a cup of tea)

RENAULT
I rang for you about an hour ago. Were you out?
PROSPER
(After a pause)
Yes. For a few minutes, sir. On an errand.
RENAULT
I don't recall asking you to go anywhere.
PROSPER
It—it was for myself, sir.
(He hands a cup of tea to gentleman)
RENAULT
Whatever it was—you didn't wash up carefully, did you, Pro-
sper?
(He takes a sip of tea)
PROSPER
What do you mean, sir?

RENAULT

If I observed correctly, your fingernails seem stained with something red.

PROSPER

(Looking hastily at his hand)

I—I'm sorry, sir. Accidentally I broke a bottle of wine. Pardon me for being so clumsy.

RENAULT

It's of no consequence, really.

(Takes another sip of tea)

It was very loyal of you, Prosper, to assist me—in preparing Juliet for her last sleep.

PROSPER

(Humbly)

It was a way to pay my respects to her, sir.

RENAULT

Lying there she looked like a lovely princess, didn't she?

PROSPER

Indeed she did. That was a beautiful silk gown. As I recall, she wore that many years ago.

RENAULT

Juliet wore that to her first ball. It was one of the few happy occasions that she could enjoy.

PROSPER

And those jewels were magnificent. All presents from you, as I remember.

RENAULT

(Nods)

It was my wish that no one else should ever wear them.

PROSPER

The fire is dying down. It's getting cold in here. Let me help you to bed, sir.

RENAULT

Not yet. It will be difficult for me to sleep this night.

(He puts tea cup on table)

PROSPER

You must take care sir, or you will bring some illness on yourself.

RENAULT

(Irritably)

Stop hovering over me. Go to bed yourself.

PROSPER

If you so wish it. Goodnight, sir.

(He crosses up)

RENAULT

Goodnight.

PROSPER

(Turns)

Be sure to ring if you need me.

(RENAULT nods. PROSPER exits off up left. The distressed man sighs, rises, and crosses slowly to a window and looks out).

(Sound of wind)

RENAULT

(Softly)

Sleep peacefully, my daughter.

(He turns away, crosses to fireplace and rubs his hands)

(Sound: A bell rings off left)

RENAULT

(Annoyed)

A plague on it. Who could be calling at this hour?

(Sound: A bell rings again)

RENAULT

(Crosses up)

Why doesn't Prosper answer?

(Calls)

Prosper! Prosper! I declare, the man is getting more deaf by the hour—but he will never admit it.

(Sound: Bell rings more insistently this time)
RENAULT

Confound it! I must answer it myself.
(The man picks up the lighted candle from table and crosses left to doorway. He hesitates a moment apprehensively, then by pantomime he partially opens the door)
RENAULT

(Tremulously)
Yes. Who—who is there?
JULIET

(Off)
Please let me in.
RENAULT

I ask again. Who is there?
JULIET

It is I, Father.

(RENAULT steps back in terror, as he gestures with hand as if to drive the phantom away)
RENAULT

No, it can't be! Go away! Go away!

(A pale, trembling girl enters. RENAULT nervously places candle on table)

(Sound of wind)
RENAULT

(Again the same hand gesture)
Don't come near me—whatever you are.
JULIET

Please don't be alarmed, Father.
RENAULT

Don't call me that. I buried my daughter today.

(JULIET *hurries over to fireplace and warms herself*)

JULIET

That I discovered—much to my horror.

RENAULT

Then what are you? A phantom?

(JULIET *doesn't reply as she rubs hands together facing fireplace*)

Answer me. What wickedness have I done to bring such punishment?

(JULIET *takes a few steps toward him.* RENAULT *repeats the same hand motion*)

JULIET

(Gently)

Please sit down, Father.

RENAULT

You—you insist on calling me that. I told you, my daughter Juliet is dead.

(JULIET *moves toward him. He sinks into easy chair*)

JULIET

As you see, Father, I'm standing beside you.

RENAULT

But—but it can't be. Even when Doctor Peron stated that life had passed from her body, I sat by her side for a day and a night.

JULIET

(Sits on chair near him)

I don't know what happened—but somehow life came back. *(She lifts her right hand to reveal a crimson stain on it)* Perhaps because blood began to flow.

RENAULT

Blood? How dreadful. Your hand is injured.

JULIET

It's my finger. Something caused it to bleed. I guess that revived me.

RENAULT

How strange.

JULIET

As you see, the ruby ring that I wore is gone.

RENAULT

(After·a pause, emotionally moved)

Oh, my dear! Then—then you are human. A spirit cannot bleed. Come here, my child.

(JULIET rises and kneels beside him)

My dear Juliet. Forgive me for doubting you.

(They embrace. He trembles and sobs)

JULIET

Of course, Father. I'm sorry this is such a frightening experience for you.

RENAULT

And a miracle. But how could you escape, my dear? The coffin lid seemed to fit so tight.

JULIET

When I awoke it was partly open.

RENAULT

Some rogue tampered with it. And you walked away from the graveyard?

JULIET

(Nods as she rises)

I'm glad it was nearby.

(She crosses to table)

Let's have some tea. I'll ring for Prosper.

(Picks up handbell and rings it)

RENAULT

You must be chilled to the marrow. Do you feel ill, my dear?

JULIET

A little tired. And I should bandage my finger.

RENAULT

Call Annette to do it. If she's asleep awaken her.

JULIET

I can manage it, Father.

(She crosses up a few steps, turns)

Tell Prosper to stir up the fire.

(JULIET *exits up left.* RENAULT *sinks back in his chair and closes his eyes. A moment later* PROSPER *enters with several logs*)

PROSPER

(Cautiously)
Are you asleep, sir?
(RENAULT *shakes his head*)
Did you ring, sir?
(RENAULT *nods*)
Sorry if you had to wait. I was outside gathering logs for the fireplace.
(He crosses to fireplace with logs)

RENAULT

Hurry, Prosper. Kindle a warm fire.

PROSPER

(Doing so in pantomime)
Yes, sir.

RENAULT

A miracle has happened, don't you agree?

PROSPER

What do you mean, sir?

RENAULT

That our Juliet has come back from the dead.
(PROSPER *stands transfixed*)
Don't stand there like an idiot. Go and fetch a warm wrap for her.

PROSPER

For — for whom, sir?

RENAULT

Juliet. Didn't you see her in the hallway?

PROSPER

I saw no one, sir.

RENAULT

Well, as I said, a miracle brought her back.

PROSPER

(Humoring him)

I—I'm afraid you have a fever, sir. Allow me to take you to bed—and by morning you'll feel better.
                    RENAULT
I'm not suffering from hallucinations, if that's what you mean. Somehow my daughter woke and walked from the graveyard. *(Trying to compose himself)*
It—it has upset me. Yet it is a time to rejoice.
                    PROSPER
Of course it is, sir.

                    RENAULT
What a frightful experience for her. We must do everything we can to make her comfortable.
                    PROSPER
Certainly, sir. But you're exhausted. Let me put you to bed and—
                    RENAULT
(Interrupts)
Bring in a pot of tea at once. Juliet and I will share it.

(JULIET returns from up left. She is wearing a heavy shawl and her finger is bandaged)
                    PROSPER
If—if you say so, sir. But may I—
(He stops, aware of JULIET'S presence)
                    JULIET
Good evening, Prosper. The fire is blazing nicely, thank you.

(PROSPER freezes as he stares at JULIET)
                    RENAULT
You see, Prosper. Our princess has returned.
(PROSPER is immovable)
Don't stand there gaping like an imbecile. Welcome her.
                    JULIET
(With a tolerant smile)
I understand, Prosper. The sight of me must be a shock.
                    PROSPER
It—it's incredible.

RENAULT

(Cheerfully)
Nevertheless it has happened.
(He holds out hand)
Come here, my child.
(JULIET crosses to him)
Your hand feels better now that it's bandaged?
(JULIET nods)
Very odd that your ring disappeared.
(JULIET sits on chair)

PROSPER

(Eager to leave)
Pardon me. I'll get the tea.

JULIET

There's no hurry, Prosper. I'm quite warm now.

PROSPER

But I should—

JULIET

(Interrupts firmly)
Please stay.
(She turns to her father)
Tell me, Father, was I wearing any other jewelry?

RENAULT

Yes, my dear. A gold bracelet—and the necklace that I
brought from Venice. You were so fond of them.

JULIET

I'm so sorry. As you can see, they're gone.

RENAULT

Perhaps you lost them coming back in the dark.

JULIET

Perhaps. Prosper will go and look for them in the morning.
(She turns to servant)
Won't you, Prosper?

PROSPER

(Baffled)
Well, really, I—I—

JULIET

What is it, Prosper? Has seeing me again upset you so much?

PROSPER

I—I admit I'm startled, mademoiselle. And—delighted, of course.

JULIET

Really? And are you pleased that someone didn't put the coffin lid back in place?

PROSPER

(Startled)

What? I—I don't understand, mademoiselle.

RENAULT

Juliet dear. What are you saying?

JULIET

I was awakened by a sharp pain—like a knife cutting my finger. Then I saw a man bending over me. I recognized the face.

RENAULT

Who was it, my child?

(He notices JULIET'S *accusing look to* PROSPER. *Unbelieving)*

Oh, no. It couldn't be. You're mistaken.

(Still glancing at PROSPER*)*

JULIET

No, Father. I accuse him.

RENAULT

But I trust Prosper completely. He's been my valet for over twenty years. How could he—

JULIET

(Interrupts)

But he did. It was he who opened my coffin and stole my jewelry.

RENAULT

(After a pause)

Prosper, what have you to say?

PROSPER
(Terrified)
I—I meant no harm, sir. I—I—
(He gasps for breath then collapses on the floor)

(RENAULT rises, crosses to PROSPER, kneels, and quickly examines the stricken man. He rises)
RENAULT
Guilt has taken his life. Yet I am thankful to the scoundrel. His crime brought my daughter back from the dead.

(The three characters hold their positions as the lights dim on the sitting room area)

(NARRATOR returns from down right with death masks by his side)
NARRATOR
(To audience)
And so concludes our weird tale. Death claimed Prosper for his evil doing. After that episode Monsieur Renault and his daughter visited various health resorts hoping that their health would improve, but they could never forget the ordeal of that night. They were constantly reminded of it. Monsieur Renault could never control the nervous spasm with his hand. The habit began that frightful evening when he tried to defend himself from what he believed to be a phantom. And lovely Juliet always wore a white glove to cover the scar on her finger.
(He paces a few steps)
And so, having relived this terrifying experience, with your permission the characters involved are eager to return to their haven of rest.

(NARRATOR claps his hands twice. The three people cross up center and take the same positions as before. NARRATOR returns to each of them the death mask. Each in turn holds the mask in front of face)

(The lights dim slowly to blackout)

Curtain

PRODUCTION NOTES

Properties:
 NARRATOR—Small envelope in pocket with powder in it. Death masks.
 PROSPER—Several logs.
 JULIET—Bandage on finger.
 On table—Candle in holder, matches, tea pot and cups, a handbell.

Costumes:
 NARRATOR—Neat modern attire.
 RENAULT—Robe worn over dark trousers, white shirt, and black ascot.
 PROSPER—Long frock coat, waistcoat, gray trousers, cravat.
 JULIET—Long gown of a pastel shade, a sheer scarf. Later on she wears a heavy shawl.

Light cues are indicated.

Sound: Wind and doorbell as indicated.

 The death masks worn by Renault, Juliet, and Prosper can be crude cutouts made with white or gray paper shaped to fit the faces.
 A fireplace can be constructed with heavy cardboard.

The Tell-Tale Heart

A dramatization of a short story by Edgar Allan Poe.

CAST OF CHARACTERS

MARK THOMAS — An emotional young man.
FIRST POLICEMAN
SECOND POLICEMAN

Scene — A sitting room inside a shuttered house.

Time — Winter. Several hours after midnight.

The Tell-Tale Heart

To suggest a sitting room two chairs are placed at left center. A small table is between them. An easy chair is down left of this grouping. The right area is the hallway leading to outer door which is not seen.

Sound—A police whistle. A few moments later loud raps upon the street door down right.

The raps are repeated as MARK THOMAS *wearing a robe over his pajamas and slippers on his bare feet enters from down left and hurries toward the door. He carries a lighted lantern.*

THOMAS

(Calls)
Who is it? Who is there?
FIRST POLICEMAN
(Off)
Police officers. Will you open the door?
THOMAS
Just a minute—until I unbolt the door.
(He pantomimes opening the door)

(Sound—Wind is heard off right)

FIRST POLICEMAN
Sorry to disturb you. May we come in?
THOMAS
(Politely)
Please do.

(Two burly POLICEMEN *enter a few steps)*
SECOND POLICEMAN
(Rubbing his hands)
It's cold and windy out there.
THOMAS
Won't you step inside? It's drafty here in the doorway.

(They cross toward left a few steps)

FIRST POLICEMAN
Are you the owner of this house?

THOMAS

No. This is Mr. Preston's house.

FIRST POLICEMAN

And what is your name?

THOMAS

Thomas. Mark Thomas. But may I ask what brings you here? This is a most respectable neighborhood.

FIRST POLICEMAN

Someone nearby heard a scream and notified us. Did you hear anything unusual—within the last hour or so?

THOMAS

No.

SECOND POLICEMAN

There may be a prowler about. Sometimes they break in. Do you mind if we look around?

THOMAS

Not at all. Follow me, gentlemen. As you see, we don't have many lamps about. Mr. Preston prefers to live frugally. So I'll light the way as we go.

(THOMAS *crosses left. The* POLICEMEN *follow)*

FIRST POLICEMAN

With those shutters tightly closed, we thought your house might be deserted.

THOMAS

The house is warmer that way.

(He places lantern on table)

There. This is Mr. Preston's sitting room. Let's sit here.

(POLICEMEN sit)

Comfortable?

(FIRST POLICEMAN nods. SECOND POLICEMAN *lights a pipe)*

THOMAS

(Sits in easy chair)

Now then—any more questions?

FIRST POLICEMAN

Are you a relative—of this Mr. Preston?

THOMAS

No. I'm in his employ———or rather should say, I was. He
had a bookshop—but because of poor health—a bad
heart—he sold the business. But he kept me on—as a sort of
companion, you might say.

SECOND POLICEMAN

Anyone else here in the house?

THOMAS

No, I'm alone. Mr. Preston went to—to the country. A—a little visit with relatives. He left last evening and will be back in a
few days.

FIRST POLICEMAN

Did you notice any prowler about—earlier in the evening.

THOMAS

No. I didn't venture out. It was so cold and blustery that I
stayed indoors. I read for awhile until it became too cold
—then I retired.

SECOND POLICEMAN

About what time was that?

THOMAS

Just before midnight. I heard the clock strike the hour as I pulled up the covers.
(A pause. Then eagerly)
Gentlemen, it just occurred to me. I believe I can offer the
solution—about that scream.

FIRST POLICEMAN

We're listening.

THOMAS

(A peal of laughter)
Excuse me for laughing, but I just recall. You see, I had a
dream. I don't remember the details—but it was frightening—so that I screamed and woke up. I remember that
part—that I screamed.

SECOND POLICEMAN

It must have been powerful since it woke up a neighbor.

THOMAS

Sorry if it annoyed anyone. And I'm afraid it caused you a lot of trouble.

SECOND POLICEMAN

Well, that gives us one answer to the mystery.

THOMAS

So now you can go back to headquarters—or wherever you go from here. Sorry I have no cigars to offer you. We're not accustomed to having guests.

(He rises)

So now that you have your answer, I won't detain you further.

FIRST POLICEMAN

For the record, I think we'd better search the entire house.

THOMAS

(Appears distracted)

Uh—what—what did you say? Can you speak a little louder?

FIRST POLICEMAN

(With more volume)

I said, if you don't mind we'd like to look around further.

THOMAS

It—it's getting chilly in here. Let's leave this room and—

(He crosses right a few steps then turns to POLICEMEN *who remain seated)*

Why do you keep sitting there when—

FIRST POLICEMAN

(Interrupting)

Do you mind lighting the way as we go?

THOMAS

(More excited)

There. It's getting louder. There's a ringing in my ears. I—I think I'd better go to bed. I'm feverish.

(He hurries toward left)

So excuse me if I—

(He stops suddenly and becomes more disturbed)

Listen! Don't you hear it?

(FIRST POLICEMAN shakes his head)

You lie! You must hear it. That awful ticking—like a watch

wrapped in cotton. There it is again. It's getting louder—
louder!

SECOND POLICEMAN

We don't hear a thing. Why are you so upset?

THOMAS

(Building up emotion as he crosses to them)
Oh, why do you keep on talking? It doesn't make sense. I can't
hear you because of that terrible ticking. Go, will you? Go
quickly. Oh, why do you stare at me like that? You fancy me
mad, don't you?

SECOND POLICEMAN

(Puts his pipe away)
Your behavior isn't exactly normal.

THOMAS

(Crosses away)
Oh, if only that ticking would stop. It's beating louder
now—like a hammer striking an anvil.

FIRST POLICEMAN

Mr. Thomas, will you—

THOMAS

(Interrupts loudly)
I know what it is—that terrible ticking. Do you hear? I know
what it is. But you don't. You're a fine pair. There you
sit—two stupid officers of the law—and you find nothing.

SECOND POLICEMAN

Then suppose you tell us.

THOMAS

You fools!
(He paces about)
Yes, I will. I must. Perhaps then it will stop. Listen well. I can't
talk louder. I—I did it. I killed the old man.

FIRST POLICEMAN

Preston? You—you murdered him?

THOMAS

(Nods)
Yes.

SECOND POLICEMAN

Then he didn't go away, as you said? He was here and—

THOMAS

(Interrupts impatiently)

Oh, don't ask stupid questions. Just listen. I must talk fast so it'll stop.

(He paces left)

To do this thing has haunted me for a long time. It was well planned. For a week I practiced opening the door of his bedroom—quietly, gently. And tonight I had to do it.

FIRST POLICEMAN

Why? Was there a quarrel?

THOMAS

No. I had respect for the old man. He never did me a wrong.

FIRST POLICEMAN

Then why? Was it for money?

THOMAS

No. I didn't want his filthy gold. It was his eye. That's what made me do it.

SECOND POLICEMAN

His eye?

THOMAS

(Trembles as he recalls)

I'll always see that eye. It was like that of a vulture—pale blue with a hideous film over it. Oh! It chilled the very marrow in my bones to look on it. That's why I took his life—so I could rid myself of that evil eye forever.

(He crosses to easy chair and sits)

SECOND POLICEMAN

(After a pause)

When did all this happen?

THOMAS

After the clock struck the hour of midnight. I opened the door of his bedroom.

(He points up left)

That door there. The room was black. I opened the lantern which I carried just a little — but in doing it my hand slipped against the tin. The old man heard the noise. He sat up in bed and cried out, "Who's there?" I said nothing. For a whole hour I stood there, never moving a muscle. Then I opened the lantern a little further — and a ray of light fell upon that awful eye. It was wide open.

(He rises and crosses down left)

Oh! I'll never forget it. And then I heard a dull sound — beating — beating — beating. I knew what it was. It was the beating of the old man's heart. I couldn't stand it any longer. With a yell I threw open the lantern and leaped into the room. He cried out — only once. I — I dragged him to the floor — pulled the heavy bed on top of him — and that ended it all. In a little while he was dead — stone dead.

(Exhausted he drops on a chair)

(FIRST POLICEMAN *nods to* SECOND POLICEMAN. *They rise and walk toward him)*

(Sound — Wind is heard)

THOMAS

So now you want to examine the entire house, do you? Go ahead. See if you can find the body. When you've finished, you'll agree that I'm too clever for you.

(He rises)

Come. Let's go and —

(Stops suddenly. Fearfully)

Listen! Can't you hear it? Hark! There it is again. Louder — louder — louder! I can't stand it! I must tell!

(He quickly pushes away the easy chair and points to the floor)

There — there — where I'm pointing. Tear up the planks in the floor.

(He crosses to POLICEMEN*)*
Hurry, hurry! Hear it? Must I tell you what it is? It's the beating
of his hideous heart!

Curtain

Production Notes

Properties:
  THOMAS — A lighted lantern.
  SECOND POLICEMAN — Pipe and matches.
  POLICEMEN — Nightsticks.

Costumes:
  THOMAS — Robe over his pajamas, bedroom slippers.
  POLICEMEN — Uniforms and caps.

Sound: Police whistle, raps on door, wind effects.

Lighting — A quick blackout at finish.

The Cradle Will Rock

This adaptation is based on a short narrative by Harriet Beecher Stowe. An additional character and story line have been expanded for this dramatic presentation.

CAST OF CHARACTERS

LOIS TOOTHACRE — A tall, hardy woman
POLLY CLARK — A fidgety neighbor
SARAH WILSON — A fragile-appearing spinster

Scene — A kitchen-sitting room in a Maine house.

Time — An autumn evening some years ago.

The Cradle Will Rock

The furnishings of the room are rugged. A round table is at center. On it is a lighted oil lamp, two cups and saucers, and a sewing basket. Right and left of table are two chairs. A wooden clothestree is down right. An unseen door to the outdoors is up right. At left is a rocking chair and below it a cradle. Several logs are down left before an imaginary fireplace.

37

LOIS *is seated left at table mending a man's shirt.* POLLY *is seated right busily knitting a muffler.*

Sound—The wind is heard in the background.

POLLY

(After a few moments)
Jes' listen to that wind screechin'.

LOIS

(Calmly)
All we can do, Polly, is keep our fingers busy. Frettin' about it won' make it go away.
(They knit and stitch away a few moments)
Abner will be tickled with that muffler. It'll feel warm as a lamb.

POLLY

It's fer his birthday. Next Thursday it be. An' I hope to put around his neck myself.

LOIS

'Course ya will. I have a feelin' in my bones their ship will bring 'em back any day now.

POLLY

Oh, Lois. Ain' you a sunbeam.
(She puts down knitting and crosses up to look out window)
I get the fidgets every time yer Cal an' my Abner go out in them fishin' boats. I keep wonderin' if the tide will bring 'em back.

LOIS

Hush. Ya mustn' plague yerself with sech thoughts.
(She puts down mending)
Nothin' can put cheer in ya like another cup of tea.
(As she crosses left she glances down at cradle)
There's li'l Matt fas' asleep.

POLLY

(Crosses toward her)
Oh, pshaw! I plum forgot to bring along them ginger cookies. I baked 'em this mornin'.

(She glances fondly at the figure in cradle)
My. Sleepin' like a li'l angel. An' what a comfort he be — while
ya wait fer the wind to bring back yer man.

*(LOIS has reached down for tea kettle behind the logs and
moves back to table)*

POLLY

An' to think ya found this cradle out there on the shore — jes'
afore li'l Matt come.

LOIS

(Pouring two cups of tea)
Yer tea is better for ya when it's pipin' hot.

POLLY

(Returns to her place by the table)
I cain' forget the night of that awful storm. The wind was
howlin' somethin' fierce — like a baby cryin' out there.

(LOIS crosses and places kettle down left)

LOIS

(As she returns to table)
Polly, I jes' as soon talk 'bout somethin' else.

POLLY

(Disregarding the remark)
An' when Abner listen he hear it too. So nex' mornin' he look
aroun' — but no hide or hair of a baby. Then you find that
cradle out there an' —

LOIS

(Interrupts firmly)
Again I say, nuff of that.

POLLY

My, yer touchy about it.
(They sip their tea)

(Sound — The wind is heard again)

POLLY
I ain' seen yer sister, Sarah, fer a spell. Has she fleshed up any?
LOIS
Naw. Sarah is still scrawny as ever—an' feelin' poorly.
POLLY
(With sympathy)
Aw. A pity she never got herself a feller. But then she be sorta strange—seein' spirits aroun' that no one else can see. Guess that can scare away a man.

LOIS
Don' we all have a cross to bear? Anyhow, Sarah keeps busy doin' things at church.

(Sound—The wind is louder this time)

(POLLY glances toward the cradle and notices that it is rocking. She screams and bangs down her tea cup)

LOIS
(Startled)
Laws a-mercy, Polly. What's ailin' ya?

(Frightened, POLLY points to cradle)
LOIS
(She glances at cradle. Casually)
Aw, that. Every time the wind come up it do that. I pay it no mind.
POLLY
Mercy. It's jes' as if somebody were settin' by the cradle an' rockin' it.

LOIS
(Firmly)
Now Polly, don' have a fit jes' because—
POLLY
(Interrupts)
It's spooky, I tell ya.

LOIS

Stop actin' so foolish. It ain' nothin' to get in a tizzy about.

POLLY

(Rises)

Well, I ain' gonna set here an' watch it.

(She picks up knitting and hurries over to clothestree and removes her shawl)

LOIS

(Severely)

Aw, Polly, don' be sech a fraidy cat.

POLLY

(Hotly, as she puts shawl over her head and shoulders)

'Tain' only that, Lois Toothacre. I don' like the way ya sass me back.

(She flounces toward door up right but stops suddenly)

LOIS

What now?

POLLY

Lan' sakes! Sounds as if someone is comin' by.

(LOIS rises, crosses up as SARAH WILSON enters. She is slightly built with sensitive features)

LOIS

(Pleased surprise)

Sarah! What brings ya by—when a storm is brewin'?

SARAH

Somehow I jes' felt like comin' over.

LOIS

(Crosses to SARAH)

Anyhow, glad to see ya. Ya know Polly. She live across the way.

(SARAH nods)

POLLY

Jes' been askin' about ya. But I can see yer tuckered out walkin' a mile to get here.

LOIS

(Takes SARAH'S *cape and bonnet)*
My, them things is cold.

POLLY

(Crosses toward door)
Well, I'm on my way.

LOIS

When ya get home, Polly, sing a hymn. It'll make ya feel better.

POLLY

(Saucily, at doorway)
Hmm! An' you should stitch yer tongue.
(She hurries off)

(Sound — Wind howls)

(The cradle rocks again)

LOIS

(Crosses to clothestree and hangs up wraps)
It's good ya come by. Polly an' me were 'bout to have a spat.
Now go over there by the fire an' warm yerself.

SARAH

(Crosses left)
An' li'l Matt — is he asleep?
(She notices the cradle rocking)
Oh.

LOIS

Pay no mind to that rockin'. It do that when the wind is high.
Go on, Sarah, set on that chair. I'll bring Matt fer ya to hold.
It's 'bout time for his feedin'.
(SARAH crosses toward rocking chair then stops)
What's wrong now?

SARAH

(Points to rocker)
Who — who is that woman settin' there?

LOIS

Why, sister, there ain' nobody there.

SARAH

But I see her. She's settin' there — leanin' over — an' rockin' the cradle.

LOIS

(Kindly)

Foolish talk, Sarah. Reckon that long walk in the wind done tire ya out. Go in the other room an' rest a spell.

SARAH

(Not hearing)

Her face is so sad an' pale — an' her long black hair is hangin' down.

LOIS

Now, Sarah. Come, set over here.
(She leads SARAH away and sets her left at table)

SARAH

(Her eyes still on the rocking chair)

She's wearin' a silk dress. Now she looks at me as if to say somethin'.

LOIS

(Behind the table. After a pause)

Well?

SARAH

Poor lady. Her eyes are so pitiful.

LOIS

Don' fret so. I'll bring ya a cup of tea.

SARAH

(More excited)

Now she's standin' up an' walkin' to the cradle.

LOIS

What!

SARAH

She stoops over — as if to pick up li'l Matt.

LOIS

(With spirit as she crosses to cradle)

Naw! Naw, she don'. She won' tech my baby.
(She reaches down, grasps the tiny bundle in her arms, then hurries to front of table)
Where—where is she now?

                              SARAH

The lady turns away. She's cryin'.

                              LOIS

(Angrily)
An' she should. Tryin' to steal my baby.
(She sits right at table)

                              SARAH

I pity her. Perhaps she— Oh. She—she melted away.

                              LOIS

An' she can stay away.

                              SARAH

(Faces her)
Sister, remember that awful storm—when ya found that cradle the nex' mornin'?

                              LOIS

(Nods)
It would take a heap of forgettin' not to.

                              SARAH

Mebbe a ship wen' down—an' that lady an' her baby done drown. An'—

                              LOIS

(Interrupts sharply)
Well, I don' want her back. I want no sech doin's in my house.
(Reaching a decision, she rises and crosses to SARAH*).*
Here, Sarah, take the baby.

                              SARAH

(As she takes the bundle)
Lois, what are ya doin'?

                              LOIS

(Determined, as she strides to fireplace)
I wanna be sure that spook lady won' come back.
(She picks up an ax that is beside the logs)
That cradle done rock fer the last time.

SARAH
(Rises in alarm and crosses to her)
Sister, don'! It ain' right!
(She extends a restraining hand)
LOIS
Let me be. I'm choppin' it up fer kindlin'.
(With a few strokes of the ax the cradle falls apart. Then she throws pieces in the fireplace)
There. Let it burn. An' the spook lady with it.

(SARAH moans as LOIS takes baby from her and crosses to her chair by table. SARAH slowly returns to her chair by table and sobs softly. For a few moments the women sit there. LOIS is patting the baby as her body rocks)

(Sound—A baby's cry is heard from fireplace area)
LOIS
(Alarmed)
Sarah, ya hear that?
(SARAH, still sobbing, nods)
It come from the fire.

(Sound—The baby's cry becomes louder over the sound of wind)
LOIS
(She trembles with fright)
Laws a-mercy! How that poor baby is cryin'!

(Lights—Dim to blackout)

Curtain

Production Notes

Properties:
  LOIS—Man's woolen shirt. Needle and thread.

POLLY — Knitting (muffler).

On table — Table cover, sewing basket, two cups, two saucers.

On clothestree — A large shawl.

Behind logs — Tea kettle with liquid.

In cradle — Doll wrapped in blanket.

At fireside — Ax.

Costumes:

LOIS — Dark housedress with long sleeves.

POLLY — Plain housedress, shawl.

SARAH — Light colored, plain dress, bonnet, cape.

Sound: Wind effects and baby crying.

A break-away cradle can be constructed with heavy cardboard.

A string that extends off-stage left is attached to cradle to make it rock when indicated.

Nobody's House

This play is adapted from the short story of the same name by A. M. Burrage.

CAST OF CHARACTERS

MR. ROSS — A gray-haired, troubled gentleman
MRS. PARK — A tall, gaunt, middle-aged woman

Scene — The hallway and library in a vacant house.

Time — Dusk on a windy, autumn evening.

Nobody's House

The right area is the hallway. Down right is an opening that leads to kitchen. Up right is an invisible street door. A sittable stool and a chair with a wooden crate between them are downstage. The center and left area is a vacant library. A few logs down left suggest a fireplace. A low stool and an empty crate are nearby.

STEPHEN ROSS *enters a few steps from up right and pushes an imaginary bell.*

Sound—The door chime rings.

He wears a cape or loose-fitting outer coat over his suit, and a black hat that is pulled down over his forehead.

After a moment MRS. PARK, *carrying a lighted lamp, enters from down right. She places lamp on crate, wipes her hands on a long apron, then crosses up to door and pantomimes opening it.*

Sound—Wind.

MR. ROSS
(Gravely)
Good evening, ma'am.
(He takes a note from his pocket)
I have a note here from the real estate office allowing me to see the house.

MRS. PARK
(Annoyed as she glances at note)
Oh. I was just fixin' some supper

MR. ROSS
I'm sorry. I won't keep you long.

MRS PARK
Step in, Mr. Ross.
(She backs away as he steps in. He walks with a slight limp)
You won't see the house at its best. There's nothin' in it but a few sticks of furniture. I have to show you it by this lamp. The electric light is shut off.

MR. ROSS
You live here?

MRS. PARK
(She nods, then indicates to right)
I make do in that large kitchen over there. I've been caretaker ever since the house became empty.

MR. ROSS
Has it been empty a long time?

MRS. PARK

Almost twenty years. This is supposed to be a fine hall—and that staircase is elegant.
(With a quick glance toward left)
There's the library. But hardly anyone stops by now. This place is too large for most people. I call it nobody's house.
(She observes that her caller is shivering)
You seem to be cold.

MR. ROSS

Yes. I had a long trip on the train. Could I trouble you for a cup of tea?

MRS. PARK

The kettle is on.
(She crosses right, then turns and indicates the chair)
May as well make yourself comfortable.
(She exits)

MR. ROSS

Thank you.
(He looks about, takes off hat, walks to chair and sits)

(MRS. PARK returns with a tray on which are cups, saucers, and a pot of tea)

MRS. PARK

(As she moves toward crate)
I'll have a cup with you, if you don't mind.
(She puts tray on crate and busies herself pouring tea).

MR. ROSS

Please do. Tell me, do you live here alone?

MRS. PARK

Yes.
(She sits on stool)

(Sound—Wind comes up)

MR. ROSS

This house—to whom did it belong?

MRS. PARK

A gentleman named Philip Fraser.
(Holding a cup, she turns her head a little to one side as if listening)

MR. ROSS

Do you hear anything?

MRS. PARK

(Slightly flustered)
No, just the wind.
(Hands him a cup)
Here's your tea.

MR. ROSS

Thank you. May I ask, do you ever hear things?

MRS. PARK

Hear things? No. Why should I?

MR. ROSS

Sometimes in these empty old houses strange things happen.

MRS. PARK

(Pauses, as she deliberately changes the subject)
Help yourself to milk and sugar.

MR. ROSS

This man Fraser — is he still alive?

MRS. PARK

(Wary)
I couldn't say.

MR. ROSS

Didn't some scandal happen in this house?

MRS. PARK

I don't know.

MR. ROSS

Forgive me. I think you do.

MRS. PARK

(After a pause)
There are stories.

MR. ROSS

(Gently)
Tell me.

MRS. PARK

I can't, sir. If I told people I'd lose my job. They'd think I was preventin' people from takin' this house.

MR. ROSS

It wouldn't prevent me. Wasn't this Fraser supposed to have shot —

MRS. PARK

(Breaks in as she puts down her cup)
Oh. Then you heard.

MR. ROSS

A little. Please tell me all. It will not affect me as a prospective buyer, I assure you.

MRS. PARK

(Passes a hand across her forehead)
I don't like talkin' about it. You see, I live here alone and —

MR. ROSS

(Interrupts)
And you sometimes hear noises? Tell me — what kind of noises?

MRS. PARK

Oh, it's imagination. Sometimes the wind sounds like footsteps and voices. Or a loose door somewhere that bangs.

MR. ROSS

(Leaning forward he scarcely speaks above a whisper)
You mean, you hear a shot fired?

MRS. PARK

It — it does sound like that.

MR. ROSS

You believe this house is haunted, don't you?

MRS. PARK

When there's been a tragedy in a house, people will say anythin'.

MR. ROSS

Never mind what people say. What do you say?

MRS. PARK

(Sullenly)
I don't know. I've heard things. I tell myself they're nothin'.
(Gropes for a handkerchief from apron pocket)

I have to tell myself they're nothin'.
(She dabs her face with handkerchief)

                    MR. ROSS
(In a low, strained voice)
Then you haven't seen anything?

                    MRS. PARK
No, thank God. I never go near the library after dark.

                    MR. ROSS
Why not? Please tell me.

                    MRS. PARK
(Gulps some tea as if to give her courage)
Well, I heard about it a long time ago — when Philip Fraser lived here. He had a young wife, Muriel. He was mad about hun-
tin' — and had a large stable of horses. The three of them would
often go out ridin'. He and his wife — and Paul Marsh, a good
friend of Mr. Fraser's.

                    MR. ROSS
Go on.

                    MRS. PARK
One day he took a bad fall and broke his leg. It took a long
time to heal — so he started gettin' strange moods. That didn't
stop his friend and his wife from seein' each other. But nobody
seems to know if Mr. Fraser was jealous.
(She rubs her hands nervously)
Oh, I shouldn't be tellin' you this.

                    MR. ROSS
Believe me, you should.

                    MRS. PARK
One day when they were out followin' the hounds, Mr. Fraser
was sittin' in the library cleanin' his revolver. When the two
came back, his wife went upstairs. His friend came into the
library to get himself a whiskey. Then angry words were heard
and a shot was fired. When the butler burst into the room he
found Paul Marsh lyin' dead — and Mr. Fraser sittin' in his
chair before the fire — with a revolver in his hand.

MR. ROSS

(His head is bent)
That is all you remember?

MRS. PARK

He pleaded not guilty at the trial—sayin' his mind was a blank
when the shot was fired. But the jury found him guilty.

MR. ROSS

(Glancing at her earnestly)
And you—do you think he did it?

MRS. PARK

(Taken aback)
Of course. There was only those two in the room.

MR. ROSS

(Quietly)
I don't believe he did it. I knew the man.

MRS. PARK

What!

MR. ROSS

(Rises, takes a few steps up and back)
I knew him well—as a boy—and a man. They say he had fits of
madness—but mad or sane—he couldn't have done it. He lov-
ed his wife—and Paul Marsh was his best friend.
(Notices her expression)
But I'm frightening you. I don't mean to. But there he is rot-
ting in prison and doesn't know if he's innocent or guilty.

MRS. PARK

(Alarmed)
Why have you come here? You don't want this house.

MR. ROSS

(Crosses to her)
No. I came here as his friend—to find out.

MRS. PARK

(Draws back)
What?

MR. ROSS

They say strange things happen in the library. And you tell me

that you hear footsteps and the sound of a shot. Perhaps it is
Paul Marsh who returns.

MRS. PARK

(Sharply, as she rises)
I can't let you go in the library.

MR. ROSS

I must. I'm going to spend the night there.

MRS. PARK

It's madness. No one has entered that room after nightfall.

MR. ROSS

I will!

MRS. PARK

I shall be discharged if it's found out.

MR. ROSS

It won't be found out.
(He reaches in breast pocket for wallet)
I came here to pay for the privilege.
(He hands her several bills)
Here, take these and act like a sensible woman.

MRS. PARK

I'm doin' wrong.

MR. ROSS

(Pressing bills into her hand)
You're doing right. I'll get the truth tonight if I have to sum-
mon the Devil himself.
(He turns toward library)
Is there any furniture in there?

MRS. PARK

No.

MR. ROSS

Then if I may, I will take this chair.
(He lifts chair)

*(*MRS. PARK *picks up lamp from crate and moves to library as*
MR. ROSS *follows)*

MR. ROSS

It's cold in here.

MRS. PARK

(Walks to crate and puts lamp on it)
I'll light those logs in the fireplace.
(She crosses to logs)

MR. ROSS

(After looking about room indicates the right wall of library)
There's a hole in one of these panels.

MRS. PARK

(Kneeling, pantomimes lighting the fire)
Yes. It's a bullet hole. It lodged there after—

MR. ROSS

(Interrupts)
I understand.
(He places chair near fireplace, then sits down facing library door)
And that afternoon, over twenty years ago, I was sitting here—

MRS. PARK

(Alarmed, she rises)
You were sittin' there? Then you ain't Mr. Ross! You're Philip Fraser, the murderer!

MR. ROSS

(Quietly)
Murder or not—only God knows. But I shall learn tonight. Thank you for lighting the fire. You may leave now.

MRS. PARK

(Distressed, as she hurriedly moves away)
I shall never forgive myself for doin' this.
(When she arrives at the other side of library door, she bends over to listen)

(MR. ROSS draws the stool near him and props his injured leg on it. Then he reveals a revolver from his coat pocket)

(Sound—Wind is heard for a moment)

MR. ROSS

(Calls, as he faces library door)

Paul. Paul, can you hear me? I'm sitting in the same place that I sat that evening, with my bad leg resting on a stool. And here's that damn revolver. Did I shoot you, Paul? My mind is a blank. For twenty years I've tried to remember.

(A pause. Then he speaks more desperately)

Is it because you hate me that you don't appear? You do come back. They all say so. That woman hears you walking about. You — in your scarlet coat, as you came in that evening. I was sitting here — when you both came back. I heard you in the hall. Muriel was laughing at something. Then she went upstairs and I thought, "She doesn't come in to see me. I'm nothing to her now that I'm crippled. She loves Paul. I've been blind as well as lame. The things I've seen which they pretended were nothing. The things I haven't seen, but heard of in whispers." Then my brain caught fire and you came in.

(Sound — Wind is heard)

MR. ROSS

(A hoarse cry)

Paul! Paul, I see you! Oh, God, I'm beginning to remember. You stood where you're standing now — touching the handle of the door. And you said — I remember now. "Give me a shot of whiskey, Phil. I'm frozen." Paul, don't look like that! I'm remembering.

(He aims pistol toward doorway)

Damn you! When you turned your back on me like that, I —

(He fires)

(Sound — Revolver shot)

(Agitated, MRS. PARK *hurries toward street door)*

(Breathing heavily, MR. ROSS *points gun toward himself and fires. He collapses on floor)*

(Sound—Revolver shot)

(At doorway, MRS. PARK *gives a fearful look toward library, then turns and hurries off)*

MRS. PARK

(Screaming hysterically as she hurries off)
Police! Police! Police!

(Sound—Wind comes up again)

Curtain

PRODUCTION NOTES

Properties:
   MRS. PARK—A lighted lamp. Tray with tea service for two,
           milk and sugar. Handkerchief in apron pocket.

   MR. ROSS—A note.
           Wallet with money.
           Revolver.

Costumes:
   MRS. PARK—House dress with a large apron.
   MR. ROSS—Business suit with cape or loose-fitting outer coat,
           black hat.

Sound: Door chime. Wind as indicated. Revolver shots. A realistic cap pistol can be used. Or a sound effect of a pistol shot can be done. It can also be simulated by striking a leather cushion with a stick offstage.

Lighting: Only playing areas are well lighted.

The Canterville Ghost

A dramatization of the short story with the same title by Oscar Wilde. To accent the humor of this episode, the style of acting should be slightly overplayed.

CAST OF CHARACTERS

LORD CANTERVILLE — An aristocratic British gentleman
HIRAM OTIS — An American minister
MRS. OTIS — An attractive, dignified lady
WASHINGTON OTIS — A mischievous lad of 17
VIRGINIA OTIS — A golden-haired lass of 15
MRS. UMNEY — A loyal housekeeper
GHOST OF SIMON CANTERVILLE — A gray haired, forlorn specimen of a man
DUKE OF CHESHIRE — A handsome specimen of royalty

Scene — Inside a mansion in England.

Time — A span of a summer in the 1890s.

The Canterville Ghost

No setting is necessary. Two chairs are placed up center. Another chair is down right.

58

LORD CANTERVILLE *appears from down left. He is pompous in manner.* MR. *and* MRS. OTIS *and their children,* WASHINGTON *and* VIRGINIA, *are arranged in a family pose up center. The parents are seated on chairs and their children are standing behind them in a frozen position.* LORD CANTER- VILLE *steps front and addresses the audience.*

LORD CANTERVILLE

(With a pronounced British accent)

Being a man of punctilious honor, ladies and gentlemen, I have to admit that my former mansion, Canterville Chase, is haunted. We never cared to live there since my great-aunt, the Dowager Duchess of Bolton, was frightened into a fit by two skeleton hands being placed on her as she was dressing for din- ner. After that unfortunate incident, none of the servants would stay with us. My wife, Lady Canterville, slept very little at night because of mysterious noises that came from the cor- ridor and the library. I explained all this to Hiram Otis, an American minister.

(With a flourish of his hand he indicates the group at center. He crosses toward group)

Mr. Otis has a very determined jaw which indicates a strong will. Mrs. Otis had been a celebrated New York belle. As you can observe, she has a magnificent constitution. In fact, she is an excellent example of what we in Britain have in common with America — except, of course, the language. Standing behind her is their son. In a moment of patriotism he was christened Washington, which later caused regret. The young man despises the name and for revenge has become an ex- cellent ballroom dancer. And there is Miss Virginia Otis, age fifteen, looking lovely as a fawn. She can race around the park like an Amazon.

(He crosses toward left)

But to return to the business proposition. I even stated to Mr. Otis that he was doing a very foolish thing to purchase the place.

(MR. OTIS *steps away from group and crosses toward* LORD CANTERVILLE)

MR. OTIS

My Lord Canterville, I will take the furniture and the ghost at a valuation. I come from a modern country where we have everything that money can buy. If there was such a thing as a ghost in Europe, we'd have it in America in one of our museums — or take the ghost on the road as a show.

LORD CANTERVILLE

I insist, sir. The ghost does exist and has been well-known for three centuries. He makes an appearance before the death of any member of our family.

MR. OTIS

So does the family doctor. I still affirm, Lord Canterville, there is no such thing as a ghost.

LORD CANTERVILLE

Very well, Mr. Otis. It's apparent that you don't mind a ghost in the house. But remember you were sufficiently warned.

(MR. OTIS *returns to the family group*)

LORD CANTERVILLE

The transaction was concluded and the Otis family came to England that summer. Mrs. Umney, the housekeeper, was there to greet them.

(MRS. UMNEY *enters from down right and crosses toward center as the Otis family moves in that direction.* LORD CANTERVILLE *crosses up left a few steps*)

MRS. UMNEY

(With a low curtsy)
I bid you welcome to Canterville Chase.

MR. OTIS

Thank you.

MRS. OTIS

You must be Mrs. Umney. How nice of you to be here and welcome us.

MRS. UMNEY

Perhaps you'd like a spot of tea. It's ready in the library.

MRS. OTIS

A little later, thank you. If you don't mind, we'd like to look around. The children are bursting with curiosity to see every corner of the place.

MRS. UMNEY

Very well, madam. This way, please.

(They all cross toward the left following MRS. UMNEY*)*

MRS. UMNEY

This is Tudor Hall. We shall now enter the library.

MR. OTIS

Look at that stained glass window, Lucretia.

MRS. OTIS

Yes, Hiram. It's lovely.
(She glances at the floor)
Oh.
(She points)
I'm afraid something has been spilled there.

MRS. UMNEY

(In a low voice)
Yes, madam. Blood has been spilled on that spot.

MRS. OTIS

How awful. I don't care for bloodstains in my sitting room.

MRS. UMNEY

(With pride)
That is the blood of Lady Eleanor de Canterville. She was murdered on this very spot by her own husband, Sir Simon de Canterville, in 1575.

VIRIGINIA

(Thrilled)
How exciting. A real murder in our house.

MRS. OTIS

Hush, dear. You were saying, Mrs. Umney.

MRS. UMNEY

Sir Simon disappeared suddenly but his body has never been discovered. His guilty spirit still haunts the Chase.

MR. OTIS

Ridiculous.

MRS. UMNEY

Not at all. That bloodstain has been admired by tourists.

MR. OTIS

I rather like it myself.

MRS. OTIS

(With spirit)

Well, I don't. It must be removed at once.

MRS. UMNEY

The stain can never be removed, madam.

MRS. OTIS

Never?

WASHINGTON

(Stepping toward MRS. UMNEY*)*

Yes, it can. All that is nonsense.

MRS. UMNEY

I beg your pardon.

*(*WASHINGTON *holds up a small stick that appears like a white lipstick)*

WASHINGTON

Pinkerton's Champion Stain Remover will clean it up in no time.

(He falls on his knees and applies stick to the spot)

MRS. UMNEY

(Horrified)

Oh, young man. You mustn't tamper with it.

WASHINGTON

(Looking pleased)

There. I knew Pinkerton would do it.

(He rises and the family smiles approval)

(Sound—A peal of thunder)

(They all react to the sound)
MRS. OTIS
Mercy. It seems as if the heavens disapprove of what you did, Washington.
MR. OTIS
I guess the country is so overpopulated that they don't have enough decent weather for everybody.

(MRS. UMNEY faints in MR. OTIS'S arms. He appears very uncomfortable supporting her)
MRS. OTIS
Oh, my. It seems we have a housekeeper who faints at a clap of thunder.

MR. OTIS
(Struggling with the weight of MRS. UMNEY)
Why didn't she do this sitting down?
MRS. OTIS
Oh, Hiram. Suppose she does this all the time?
MR. OTIS
Deduct it from her wages. That will cure her. Every time she faints or breaks a dish, we'll deduct a certain sum.

(MRS. UMNEY arouses herself)
MRS. UMNEY
(Confused)
Oh. Did I— So sorry.
(She steps aside and arranges her dress)
MRS. OTIS
There. She seems to be coming out of it. I wonder if she heard what you said.

MR. OTIS
Of course she did. Mark my words she won't faint again.

(The OTIS family freeze in position. LORD CANTERVILLE steps down and again speaks to audience)

LORD CANTERVILLE

Mrs. Umney never did repeat that performance.
(Addresses her)
You may attend to your duties now, Mrs. Umney.

*(*MRS. UMNEY *bows to him and exits down right)*

LORD CANTERVILLE

The next morning when the Otis family came down to
breakfast they found the terrible stain of blood once again on
the floor.

(The OTIS *family react again)*

WASHINGTON

It wasn't the fault of Pinkerton. I have tried the stuff with
everything. It must be the ghost.
*(Again he squats and rubs the spot with the detergent. Then he
rises)*

(The OTIS *group crosses toward two chairs up center and
assumes positions held at opening)*

LORD CANTERVILLE

The third morning the spot was there again — even though the
library had been locked up at night by Mr. Otis himself and
the key carried upstairs. This happening caused him to suspect
that he had been too dogmatic in his denial of the existence of
ghosts. That night he was awakened by a curious noise in the
corridor outside his room. It sounded like the clank of metal.

*(*GHOST OF SIR SIMON, *dressed in ragged clothes, his long gray
hair falling over his shoulders, enters from down right. Chains
hang from his wrists and ankles.* MR. OTIS *crosses toward him)*

MR. OTIS

Oh. Here you are.

(Startled at first by the pathetic appearance of the GHOST, *he is quickly in command of the situation)*
My dear sir, those chains make an awful racket. I insist you oil them.
(He extends a bottle toward the GHOST*)*
Here. I brought you a small bottle of Tammany Rising Sun Lubricator. One application should be sufficient. But I will be happy to supply you with more should you require it.
(He thrusts the bottle in the hand of the GHOST *and returns to others. He sits on chair up center)*

(The GHOST *stands motionless for a moment then dashes the bottle violently upon the floor. He turns and clanks toward right.* WASHINGTON *picks up a pillow from behind chair and tosses it toward the* GHOST. *It zooms past his head)*

GHOST

Oh. How dare they!
(He sinks wearily on chair down right)
Never in my brilliant career of three hundred years, have I been so insulted. My talent for creating terror was unsurpassed. Didn't I frighten the Dowager Duchess into a fit as she stood before the mirror in her lace and diamonds? Four of the housemaids became hysterical when I merely grinned at them. Another terrible night the wicked Lord Ashley was found in his dressing room choking on a card — the knave of diamonds. He confessed just before he died that he had cheated Charles James Fox of 50,000 pounds by means of that very card. I made him swallow it. And what a commotion I caused one lovely June evening by playing nine-pins with my bones upon the tennis court. These were some of my celebrated performances.
(He rises and paces wearily)
And now these wretched Americans come here and offer me Rising Sun Lubricator and throw a pillow at my head. No ghost in history has ever been treated so despicably. But I shall have my revenge, mark my word.

(He stamps off down right)

LORD CANTERVILLE
The next morning the Otis family discussed the subject of Sir
Simon at some length.

*(The family group becomes animated but remains in same
position)*

MR. OTIS
(Turning toward them)
Please understand, I have no wish to do the ghost any personal
injury. And really, Washington, it wasn't very polite to throw a
pillow at him.

WASHINGTON
I'm sorry, Father. It was so handy.

MR. OTIS
However, if he declines to use the Rising Sun Lubricator, we
have to take his chains from him. That's final. It would be im-
possible to sleep with such a noise going on.

VIRGINIA
I looked at the spot this morning, Papa. It's purple.

WASHINGTON
It was yellow yesterday.

MRS. OTIS
Dear me, I wonder what color it'll be tomorrow.

(Again the group freezes)

LORD CANTERVILLE
The second appearance of the ghost occurred on a Sunday
night shortly after they had gone to bed. They were alarmed by
a crash in the hall.

(Sound-Crash of metal off down right)

(GHOST *enters and sits on chair down right. He is not wearing
chains)*

LORD CANTERVILLE

A suit of old armor had fallen on the stone floor. Seated near-by, with an expression of agony on his face, was the Canterville Ghost.

(He crosses up left)

GHOST

It was foolish of me to try to put on that suit of armor. I thought it would frighten them if I walked around in it. But all I got for that brilliant idea are bruises on my knees.

(Rubbing his knees. Then he appears brighter as he rises)

Ah. Perhaps this is the time for me to give a horrifying performance. I'll render my celebrated laugh—the one that resembles a gleeful demon.

(He gives forth a horrible laugh)

(WASHINGTON steps down a few steps, puts a pea shooter to his lips and aims for GHOST. Then he returns to group)

GHOST

(Reacting to sudden pain on his head)

Ooh. What was that?

(MRS. OTIS rises and steps toward him)

MRS. OTIS

(With sympathy)

Poor man—or ghost—or whatever. I'm afraid you're far from well.

(She extends a small bottle)

I brought you a bottle of Doctor Dabell's Tincture. If it's indigestion, you'll find this an excellent remedy.

(GHOST glares at her, refuses the bottle, and turns away. MRS. OTIS returns to her chair up center)

GHOST

(With a pathetic tone)

Oh, I am foiled again. That horrid woman offering me medicine—and to be attacked by a scamp with a pea shooter. *(He sinks on chair down right)*

LORD CANTERVILLE

For some days the Ghost was extremely ill and didn't stir out of his room except to keep the bloodstains in proper order. Then one day Miss Virginia passed by the Tapestry Room and noticed that the door was open. Sitting by the window and appearing very forlorn was the Ghost of Sir Simon.

VIRIGINIA

(Crosses to him)
Hello.
(GHOST appears startled)
Sorry if I frightened you.

GHOST

That's my obligation—to frighten people.

VIRGINIA

You'll be pleased to know that my brother will go to Eton tomorrow. So if you behave yourself no one will annoy you.

GHOST

It's absurd to ask me to behave myself. I must rattle my chains, groan through keyholes, and walk about at night. It's my only reason for existing.

VIRGINIA

It's no reason at all. You have been very wicked. Mrs. Umney told us the first day we arrived here, that you killed your wife.

GHOST

I admit it. But it was a purely family affair and concerned no one else. And besides, I had my reasons. My wife was very plain, she never had my ruffs properly starched, and knew nothing about cookery.
(With more gumption)
Though I did kill her, it wasn't very nice of her brothers to starve me to death.

VIRGINIA

Starve you to death? Oh, Mr. Ghost—I mean, Sir Simon. Are you hungry. Would you like a sandwich?

GHOST

No, thank you. I never eat anything now. But it is kind of you, all the same. You are much nicer than the rest of your rude and dishonest family.

VIRGINIA

(Stamping her foot)

Stop! It is you who are rude and dishonest. Who stole the paints out of my box and pretended it was that absurd bloodstain in the library?

GHOST

But I—

VIRGINIA

(Interrupts)

Let me finish. After you took all my reds you stole other colors. It was most ridiculous. Whoever heard of emerald green blood?

GHOST

What was I to do? It is very difficult to get red blood nowadays. As for color, that is merely a matter of taste. The Cantervilles have the bluest blood in England.

(With a provoked expression VIRGINIA starts to leave)

GHOST

(Pleading)

Please don't go, Miss Virginia. I am so lonely and unhappy that I don't know what to do. I want to sleep but I cannot.

VIRGINIA

That's ridiculous. You merely go to bed. Even babies know how to do that.

GHOST

I haven't slept for three hundred years. But you can help me.

VIRGINIA

I can?

GHOST

(Nods)

Did you ever read the old prophecy that appears on the library window?

VIRGINIA

Oh, often. Let's see if I remember it.
"When a golden girl can win
  Prayer from out the lips of sin,
  When the barren almond bears,
  And a little child gives away its tears,
  Then shall all the house be still
  And peace come to Canterville."

GHOST

(Pleased)
That was perfect.

VIRGINIA

But what does it mean?

GHOST

It means that you must weep with me for my sins, because I
have no tears. Pray with me for my soul because I have no
faith. And then because you have been so sweet and good, the
angel of death will have mercy on me. Will you do it, Miss
Virginia?

VIRGINIA

(After a pause she gives him a fond embrace)
Yes, poor Sir Simon. I am not afraid. I will do what you ask.

(They exchange a friendly look as they exit down right. LORD
CANTERVILLE *steps down)*

LORD CANTERVILLE

And so it happened. Because an American girl had the
courage to carry out his request — to pray and weep for his
sins — the ghost of Sir Simon went to his final rest. The old
withered almond tree blossomed as the prophecy predicted
and the house became peaceful. Then a few years later,
another special occasion took place. Miss Virginia married the
Duke of Cheshire.
(He crosses up left)

*(*MR. *and* MRS. OTIS *rise and step front with* WASHINGTON*)*

MRS. OTIS

(Beaming)

Oh, Hiram. To think that our little Virginia is now Duchess of Cheshire.

MR. OTIS

(Not impressed)

Yes, Lucretia. But I dislike titles.

MRS. OTIS

And only last week she received a coronet from the Queen.

MR. OTIS

I shall always call my son-in-law by his first name — though I'm not too fond of that. Cecil.

WASHINGTON

But on a horse Cecil is a regular Buffalo Bill.

(VIRGINIA and DUKE appear arm in arm from down right)

DUKE

Virginia, a wife should have no secrets from her husband.

VIRGINIA

Dear Cecil. I have no secrets from you.

DUKE

Yes, you have. You never told me what happened when you were alone with Sir Simon — before he died.

VIRGINIA

I never told anyone about that, Cecil.

DUKE

I know that. But you could tell your husband.

VIRGINIA

Please don't ask me, dear. I cannot tell you. Poor Sir Simon. I owe him a great deal. He made me see what Life really is and what Death signifies — and why Love is stronger than both.

DUKE

(He puts his arms around her)

Very well. You can keep your secret, Virginia dear, as long as I have your heart.

VIRGINIA

(With an adoring look)
You shall always have that, my dear husband.
(They kiss as others beam their approval)

LORD CANTERVILLE

(Crosses down a few steps)
And so a ghost has departed — love has conquered — and we have a happy ending.

Curtain

PRODUCTION NOTES

PROPERTIES:

MR. OTIS — Small bottle.
MRS. OTIS — Small bottle.
WASHINGTON — Eradicator stick, pea shooter.
GHOST — Chains on wrist and ankles.
Behind left chair up center — Pillow.

Costumes:

LORD CANTERVILLE — Prince Albert Suit.
MR. OTIS — Frock coat, waistcoat, tight trousers, cravat.
WASHINGTON — Suit of a loud pattern.
MRS. OTIS — An elegant long dress.
VIRGINIA — Becoming long dress in a pastel shade.
MRS. UMNEY — Simple long frock with apron.
GHOST — Ragged clothes almost in tatters.
DUKE — Handsome attire of tight trousers, coat, colorful waistcoat and cravat.

Sound — Thunder and crash of armor-as indicated.

Jes' A Li'l Bitty Rag

This play is based on the short story, "The Red Rag Under the Churn" by Alice Childs.

CAST OF CHARACTERS

EBEN — A simple farmer
SARY — His sharp-tongued wife
STRANGER — A man with diabolical charm

Scene — The yard that adjoins a ramshackle cabin near the Kentucky mountains.

Time — A summer afternoon.

Jes' A Li'l Bitty Rag

As the setting represents a yard cluttered with junk, all that is required is a broken-down chair that is sittable, placed left of center, a wooden butter churn at right of center, and a water bucket near it. The cabin, not seen is in the direction up left.

EBEN, a middle-aged farmer scurries on from down right and crosses excitedly toward up left.

EBEN

(Calling)
Sary! Sary! Whar in blazes be ya?

(An untidy woman in a threadbare, dirty dress shuffles out from up left)

SARY

(Unruffled, as she wipes her hands on soiled apron)
Here I be.

EBEN

Listen, woman, I got a pow'ful notion 'bout somethin'.

SARY

An' fer that ya holler like a wildcat be after ya?

EBEN

(Still excited)
I was jes' over yonder at Clint Tollivers.

SARY

That don' surprise me none. Be he willin' to trade them hogs?

EBEN

Cain't say. Clint was out in the field. I jes' seed Lizzie.

SARY

(Gives him a baleful look)
So ya whoop up a holler fer that? Ya seed Lizzie.
(She turns left)
Hmm. I got beets on the stove.

EBEN

(Impatient)
Dang it, woman. Wait, I tell ya. It was what Lizzie was doin'
that gave me this notion.

SARY

What kind of notion?

EBEN

Wal, she was fixin' to churn butter when I come by. An'—an'
then this pow'ful thing done happen.

SARY

To Lizzie?

EBEN

Naw, to that butter churn. Lizzie had jes' set down an' started
to churn the blame thing when — wang dang — thar it be — full
up with butter.

(SARY gives him a suspicious look)

I seed it happen, I tell ya. Jes' like Lizzie done put a spell on it.

SARY

That Lizzie is a strange un. Her eyes done squint like a cat.

EBEN

Wal, I jes' had to look over that thar churn fer myself. So to git
rid of Lizzie, I ask her to git me a drink of water.

SARY

Reckon it were applejack ya done drink — from the likes of that
story.

EBEN

(Unaware of her speech)

Soon as she went to git it, I teched that churn — lifted it — looked under — an' thar it be.

SARY

What?

EBEN

A li'l bitty rag.

SARY

(Scoffs)

Huh! A fool thing to see.

EBEN

Sniff all ya like. What fer reason was it thar, I sez to myself. So
I git out my knife an' cut off a piece.

SARY

What fer?

EBEN

Mebbe it kin do pow'ful things, that's what fer.

*(He eagerly takes a small piece of red flannel from his shirt
pocket)*

Here it be.

(He holds it out toward SARY)

Feel like flannel, don' it?

SARY

(Touches it gingerly)
From off Lizzie's petticoat, I 'spect.

EBEN

So I hurry an' put back the rag jes' as Lizzie come back with a glass of water. I took a couple swallers an' then I sez I agoin' to see Clint.

SARY

An' did ya?

EBEN

Naw. I come back here as fas' as all git-out. We got to try this fer ourselves. Sary, go git cream an' do some churnin' fer me.
(He crosses to butter churn)

SARY

What fer? All we got left is a few swallers.
(She turns toward house)
Them beets — they done burn up.

EBEN

(Impatiently)
Woman, go an' git what cream thar be.

SARY

(Grumbling, as she turns away)
You air teched in the haid fer sure.
(She exits up left)

(EBEN places rickety chair in front of churn. Then he removes the top of the churn and glances inside of it. SARY returns with a small pitcher)

EBEN

Hurry, Sary. Jes' think — ef it should happen fer us same as to Lizzie.
(He holds the rag in his hand)

SARY

(Points to rag with disdain)
Hmm! As ef that li'l bitty rag could —

EBEN

(Interrupts)

Don' point at it. Mebbe that do somethin' bad to it.
(He lifts churn and places rag under it)
Thar it be. Now pour in that cream, Sary. I hitched up the
churn.

                              SARY

(She shuffles toward churn and pours in cream)
Like I tol' ya. That ain't enough in here to make a splash.

                              EBEN

Set down, Sary.
(She grumbles as she does so)
Now start churnin'.

                              SARY

(Starts to churn)
Why do I set here an' listen to an ol' fool.

                              EBEN

Churn, woman, churn.

                              SARY

(Continues churning)
Ef ya think ya can wheedle me to believe that a piece from Liz-
zie's petticoat could —
(She stops churning)
Eben!

                              EBEN

What be it, Sary?

                              SARY

I declare! The blame thing is turnin' hard.

                              EBEN

(Pleased)
Already? Ding dang. Keep churnin', Sary.

(SARY churns with more effort for a moment then stops)

                              SARY

(Frightened)
Naw. I won' do it no more.
(She rises)
That pesky thing scares me. You don' mix me up with no wit-
chery.

(EBEN cautiously opens the butter churn)

EBEN

(Joyfully)
Look, Sary, it's—it's full.
(SARY peeks at it over his shoulder)
An' did ya ever see sech perty butter.

SARY

Bewitched, that's what it be.

EBEN

Mebbe so—an' mebbe it can do us a pow'ful lot of good—that li'l bitty rag. Jes' think, woman, how easy it be. We jes' put a dab of cream in there an' ding dang, it full of butter. We jes' keep doin' that—an' sell it at the village store—an' in no time we be rich. Jes' think of that, Sary.

SARY

I don' like sech talk.

EBEN

(He picks up the rag)
Look what happen jes' now—an' all because of this li'l bitty rag.

SARY

Throw the pesky thing away, Eben. It ain't no good. That Lizzie—she must be a witch.

EBEN

(Smiling)
Ef she be, then I sure am glad to know one.

SARY

(Reaching for rag)
Give that rag to me. I'll burn it in the stove.

EBEN

(He moves the rag out of her grasp)
Sary, ya talk wild. Don' ya see. It bring us good luck.
(He puts rag in his shirt pocket)
Go in, woman, an' fetch somethin' to put this butter in. I can still take it to the village afore sundown.
(He starts left a step)
Before I do, better go an' feed them hogs.

SARY

Go on, smart man. Pay me no mind. But ef ya scare up trouble
with this foolishness, 'member I done tol' ya.
(She goes off up left)

*(EBEN crosses left but stops in astonishment as a STRANGER
blocks his path. STRANGER is dressed in black and carries a
black book)*

STRANGER

(With a polite bow)
Eben Muller, I believe?

EBEN

(Nods)
But who—who—

STRANGER

(Smiles)
Who am I? Don't be impatient. You will discover that soon
enough.

EBEN

Let me pass. I got chores to do.

STRANGER

In a minute, Eben. First we have a little business matter to set-
tle.

EBEN

A business matter? But I don'—

STRANGER

(Interrupts politely)
It will just take a moment.
(He opens the book and hands it toward Eben)
Here. Sign your name in this book, if you please.
(He produces a pen)

EBEN

(Steps back)
I cain't write so well.

STRANGER

I'm not particular about that. Just sign.

EBEN

(He cautiously takes the book and opens it)
I don' read so good. My specs is inside.

STRANGER

You won't need them. Just write your name.

EBEN

(Pointing to a page)
This writin'—what does it say?

STRANGER

Never mind about that.
(Hands pen to EBEN*)*
Just sign at the bottom of the page.

EBEN

(Squinting, trying to read)
Here at the top it says—

STRANGER

(Interrupts, with a touch of impatience)
Come, come, Eben. I can't waste time. I have other calls to make.

EBEN

(Reads with an effort)
"We, an' all that we po-sess—belong to the Devil."
(Looks at STRANGER*)*
Oh! So that's who ya be.

STRANGER

(With a slight bow)
At your service. But I am in a hurry. Will you sign, please?

EBEN

(Surprised, as he looks at page)
Why here's Lizzie Tolliver's name—an' Jud Wilson—an'—

STRANGER

(Interrupts)
Certainly. All neighbors of yours. That is why you should sign, too, Eben.

EBEN

(Stubborn)
Wal, I ain't goin' ter write my name thar. I don' belong to the Devil.

STRANGER

(With a tolerant smile)
But you do, Eben. You belong to me.

EBEN

How so?

STRANGER

Did you forget already? You just took part in witchcraft.

EBEN

I did?

STRANGER

(Nods)
Remember that little red rag you stole from Lizzie Tolliver?

EBEN

But I jes' took a li'l bitty piece.

STRANGER

You took it home and put it under your butter churn, didn't you?

EBEN

Naw, I didn'. Look fer yerself. It ain't thar.

STRANGER

Of course not. You put that li'l bitty rag in your pocket.
(He points to EBEN'S shirt pocket)

EBEN

Naw, I—
(Impulsively he puts his hand to pocket, then looks surprised)

STRANGER

(With a wise smile)
What is wrong, Eben? You look pale.

(Amazed, EBEN withdraws a little red bird from his pocket)

STRANGER

Well! You are a wizard, Eben. That li'l bitty rag is now a li'l bitty red bird.

(Enraged, EBEN flings down the bird. The STRANGER laughs)

EBEN

(Angrily)

I ain' done that. That be the Devil's doin'.

STRANGER

Thank you, Eben. I thought a little sorcery would amuse you. But come, we tarry. Sign.

EBEN

(With gumption)

I ain't put my name on no page whar the Devil has his'n. I ain't no Bible readin' man but I have respect fer the Lord, an'—

STRANGER

(Interrupts, frightened)

I forbid you to mention that name.

EBEN

The Lord?

(STRANGER nods)

Afraid of him, be ya?

(With a sudden inspiration)

I done change my mind. I will sign my name—but not on this here page.

(He turns over a few pages)

Here's one with nothin' writ on it.

(He writes hurriedly)

STRANGER

Eben, I warn you! If you fail to obey me, I will—

EBEN

(Interrupts)

Thar. I done sign it.

(He reads with difficulty what he wrote)

"We an' all that we done have—belongs to the Lord."

STRANGER

(Cringing)

Don't sign that, I beg of you!

EBEN

(Continues writing)

An' I sign it. Eben Muller.

(He does so. The STRANGER *moans)*
There, Devil. I ain't afeared of ya.
(He thrusts the book to the STRANGER *who looks at it with horror)*

(Sound—A crash of thunder)

*(*STRANGER *departs quickly down left.* EBEN *appears stunned as he gazes at the ground where the* STRANGER *stood. Recovering from the shock, he hurries up left)*

                         EBEN
Sary! Sary! Come on out.

*(*SARY *appears from up left. She carries a skillet)*
                         SARY
(Irritable)
Now what?

                         EBEN
(Agitated)
Sary, I jes' spoke to the Devil.
                         SARY
(Shakes her head, unbelieving)
I declare. Now I know ya is teched for sure.
                         EBEN
Woman, I tell ya he was here.

                         SARY
(Observing him closer)
Ya do look plum beat out.

*(*EBEN *takes* SARY *by the arm and leads her down left)*

                         EBEN
Come, let me show ya.
(He points to the spot where the STRANGER *stood)*
The Devil stood there. Look, the grass is all burned off.

SARY

(Impressed)
Why, so it be.

EBEN

(Picks up the red bird)
An' this li'l bitty red bird—know what that be afore he chang-
ed it?
(SARY *shakes her head*)
That li'l bitty red rag.

SARY

Thar, I done tol' ya. It is bewitched. An' now we have
reckonin' to do with the Devil himself.

EBEN

I know. I done a wicked thing—when I stole that li'l bitty rag.
But I don' belong to no Devil—like them others.

SARY

(Puzzled)
Others? Eben, what are ya—

EBEN

(Interrupts)
He done showed me a book—an' on one page Lizzie—Jud—all
our neighbors writ on it—sayin' they belong to him.

SARY

Mercy!

EBEN

Come on, Sary, let's pack up.
(He moves away)

SARY

Pack up?

EBEN

I ain't stayin' around here—ef all them belong to the Devil.

SARY

Have you no gumption, Eben, to let the Devil scare ya like
that. Anyhow, whar can we go?

EBEN

Over to yer Pa fer a spell. He's a Bible readin' man.

SARY

I'm stayin'. I ain't scared.

EBEN

Don' be so sure, woman. The Devil may call on you next.

SARY

How so?

EBEN

You took part in that witchery, too. Ya done crank the butter churn.

SARY

(Suddenly frightened)

Oh, Eben. You put a fright in me.

EBEN

The Devil know your name too, I reckon.

SARY

(Angrily)

An' if he do, it be your fault. It was you who done coax me, ya varmint.

(She attempts to hit him with the skillet as EBEN *hurries off. She follows him)*

Curtain

PRODUCTION NOTES

Properties:
 EBEN — A small piece of red flannel.
         A little red bird (toy).
 SARY — Small pitcher with milk. Skillet.
 STRANGER — A black book. Pen.

Costumes:
 EBEN — Tattered overalls, colored shirt, battered straw hat.
 SARY — Dark, worn house dress, large apron, shabby bedroom slippers.
 STRANGER — Black cape, black trousers, black shirt, red ascot.

Sound: Crash of thunder as indicated.

The Betrayal

A dramatic adaptation of the short story, "The Romance of
Certain Old Clothes" by Henry James.

CAST OF CHARACTERS

ROSALIND WINGRAVE—A vain, attractive young woman
PERDITA WINGRAVE—Her pretty, modest sister
MRS. WINGRAVE—A society matron
BERNARD WINGRAVE—A pleasant young man
ARTHUR LLOYD—A handsome and stylish gentleman

Scenes—Various rooms in the elegant Wingrave home.
A room in Arthur Lloyd's home in Boston.

Time—A span of several years in the 1850s.

The Betrayal

*No special scenery is required. Four chairs are up left. The
right area suggests a bedroom. A bench for an imagined dressing table is placed there. The left area suggests a parlor. A
small table with a wedding veil and a string of pearls on it is at
right. These, plus a key, are the only properties used.*

PERDITA, MRS. WINGRAVE, BERNARD *and* ARTHUR *are seated on chairs at left. Their costumes are of the Victorian era.* ROSALIND, *appearing pale, enters slowly from down right and addresses the audience.*

ROSALIND

I am the ghostly presence of Rosalind Wingrave. Because of a wrongdoing in my lifetime, as penance I must linger on earth and relive certain events in my life. As a mortal I existed in the middle of the nineteenth century. We lived in the province of Massachusetts.

(She turns toward the seated people. As their names are mentioned each acknowledges it with a slight nod of the head and then retains the frozen position)

Mrs. Wingrave, my widowed mother. . . .My sister, Perdita. . . . And my brother, Bernard. . . .who was named after my father. I was three years older than my sister, Perdita. We were so named — Perdita and Rosalind — because Father was an avid reader of Shakespeare and they appeared in two of his plays. We lived comfortably and Mama saw to it that my sister and I were taught all the accomplishments and graces comparable to the fashionable ladies of London. As for Bernard, Mama insisted that he complete his education at Oxford. He was away for five years before he returned home.

*(*BERNARD *and* ARTHUR *rise and cross toward* PERDITA *and* MRS. WINGRAVE*)*

As a surprise, he brought along a college mate, Mr. Arthur Lloyd.

BERNARD

(Brightly)
Mother, I'd like to present my chum, Arthur Lloyd.

MRS. WINGRAVE

How do you do, Mr. Lloyd. So nice you could arrange a visit with us.

ARTHUR

(With a slight bow)
My pleasure, madam.

BERNARD

And my little sister, Perdita.

PERDITA

(Shyly)
Hello.

ARTHUR

(With a slight bow)
I'm delighted.

BERNARD

I must say she has sprouted up a few inches.

MRS. WINGRAVE

Of course she has. Perdita was only fifteen when you left.

BERNARD

(Taking ARTHUR'S *arm as they cross to* ROSALIND*)*.
Come along, old boy, and meet another charmer. Rosalind,
may I present Arthur Lloyd.

ARTHUR

(With a slight bow)
It's my pleasure, Miss Wingrave.

ROSALIND

How do you do, Mr. Lloyd.

ARTHUR

I say, Bernard, you are the lucky chap—with two lovely sisters
and a charming mother.

BERNARD

I suppose so. And it's their good fortune to have me.

ROSALIND

Bernard mentioned you so often in his letters.

PERDITA

And about the many places you visited together.

BERNARD

Ah, yes. A fellow of many talents, Sir Arthur here. He speaks
French eloquently.

MRS. WINGRAVE

Oh? Then you and Rosalind can converse. She studied French
at school.

BERNARD

If you desire music — Arthur can sing an aria from an opera.

MRS. WINGRAVE

How lovely. Perdita plays the harpsichord.

BERNARD

And with a little persuasion, he can recite poetry by the hour.

ARTHUR

That will do, old boy. You make me sound like a conceited bore.

MRS. WINGRAVE

Not a bit, Mr. Lloyd. We shall look forward to such a display of talents.

BERNARD

He'll be offended if you don't ask him. But come along, Arthur. Let's go upstairs and unpack.

ARTHUR

(With a slight bow to ROSALIND*)*
If you will excuse me.
*(*ROSALIND *nods. He turns to* MRS. WINGRAVE *and* PERDITA, *with another bow)*
Ladies.

(They nod and smile. ARTHUR *and* BERNARD *exit right.* MRS. WINGRAVE *and* PERDITA *resume their frozen positions)*

ROSALIND

(To audience)
Aside from being so talented and handsome, Mr. Lloyd was rich in pounds sterling — which by no means detracted from his appeal. On many occasions we had tea in the parlor while Arthur and Bernard entertained us with stories about the interesting people they met and the fascinating places they had visited together in Europe. Arthur seemed equally attentive to Perdita and me. Secretly, I longed that he would prefer me — and I'm sure Perdita wished the same for herself. He would have to show his preference sometime. But when? I made that discovery one gray December afternoon.

(She crosses to bench and sits)
I was sitting in front of my dressing table arranging my hair.
(By pantomime she brushes hair)
It was getting dark in the room so I lit two candles.
(She lights two candles in front of her by pantomime)
Then I crossed over to the window to draw the curtain. What I
saw out in the garden disturbed me.
*(She crosses up right and about to draw curtains when she
observes something outside that surprises her. Angrily she
closes the curtain by pantomime. Appearing perturbed she
paces about)*

*(PERDITA rises from chair and hurries toward ROSALIND. She is
happily flushed and breathless)*
                         PERDITA
Oh. Here you are. I thought perhaps you and Mama had gone
to Mrs. Parker's tea party.
                         ROSALIND
We'll leave shortly.
(She crosses to bench, sits, and fixes her hair)
And where were you? A rendezvous in the garden — judging by
that pretty flush on your cheek.
                         PERDITA
The air was exhilarating.
(She turns away)
I — I want to ask Mama about something.
                         ROSALIND
(Firmly)
Stay here.
(More affable)
Help me with my hair. Will you, please?
(With no apparent interest PERDITA arranges her sister's hair)
It always appears more attractive when you do it.
(She glances at PERDITA'S hand)
Oh. A ring.
                         PERDITA
Yes. I — I just received it.

ROSALIND

Indeed. By whom?

PERDITA

(After a pause)
Arthur.

ROSALIND

(A touch of envy)
My, my. Arthur is generous all of a sudden.

PERDITA

No, Rosy, not all of a sudden. He offered it to me a month ago—but I asked him to wait until now.

ROSALIND

Really?
(A closer look at ring)
It's lovely. So that was the reason you kissed him so passionately—a few minutes ago.

PERDITA

You—you were watching?

ROSALIND

I was closing the curtain at the time.
(She turns away from mirror and faces PERDITA)
Does Mama know of this intrigue?

PERDITA

(With spirit)
Yes. She has approved of my intrigue, as you call it. And so did Bernard.

ROSALIND

(Glares at PERDITA as she rises and moves away)
So I'm the last to know.

PERDITA

(Sincerely)
I'm sorry, Rosy. I wanted to tell you but— Well, I know you're fond of Arthur, too. So—
(With forced lightness)
After all, Arthur couldn't marry both of us.

ROSALIND

(With a low curtsy)

You have my very best wishes, Perdita dear.

PERDITA

Please don't dramatize.

ROSALIND

I wish you every happines and a long life.

PERDITA

(Annoyed)

Don't speak to me in that tone. Your wishes sound false. Why don't you curse me instead?

ROSALIND

(She returns to bench, sits, speaks unemotionally)

I wish you joy—and plenty of children.

PERDITA

Thank you. And will you give me at least one year to live? In a year I can have one little boy—or one little girl.

ROSALIND

Now who is insolent? Will you please go and see if Mama is ready.

(PERDITA flounces off and returns to chair and sits in frozen position. ROSALIND *rises and crosses to position down right)*

ROSALIND

It was arranged that the wedding take place on an April day. Our house bustled with activity. Mama insisted that the bride have an elaborate trouseau. So there was a great rustling of silks, satins, velvets, and laces. That special day finally arrived. After the church ceremony the devoted couple were eager to leave and spend several days in the country. Arthur was waiting outside by the carriage while Perdita said good-by to Mama and Bernard in the parlor. I was upstairs in front of my dressing table.

(She crosses to table and picks up wedding veil and string of pearls and wears them. Then she crosses to bench, sits, and admires her reflection in the glass)

(PERDITA rises and hurries toward Rosalind)

PERDITA

Rosy, are you in there?
(She sees her)
Here you are. We're about to leave and —
(She notices that her sister is wearing bridal veil)
Oh. How — how could you?

ROSALIND

It's becoming, isn't it?

PERDITA

(Stunned)
What are you doing with — I thought you'd be downstairs to
say good-by.

ROSALIND

I kissed you good-by at church.

PERDITA

You're wearing my pearls, too.

ROSALIND

They feel so warm — as if they belonged to me.

PERDITA

A wedding gift from Arthur — as you well know.

ROSALIND

He has admirable taste.

PERDITA

(With spirit)
How can you be so brazen? I knew you were jealous of me — but
to flaunt it like this —

ROSALIND

Do you begrudge these few minutes, sister dear — when I can
pretend to be Mrs. Arthur Lloyd?

PERDITA

(She glares at ROSALIND *a moment then controls her emotions)*
Arthur is waiting.
(She crosses left a step or two)
I'll be back for my belongings — when we return from the coun-
try.
(She turns away, then back to ROSALIND*)*

You might have been decent enough to wait until I left the house.
(She hurries off down left)

ROSALIND

(She removes veil and necklace)

After a honeymoon in the country they moved into an elegant house in Boston.

(She rises, crosses to table, and places veil and necklace on it)

Nearly a year passed before we saw Arthur Lloyd again.

(She crosses down)

That was when Bernard took a wife and Arthur attended the wedding. Perdita couldn't attend. She was soon to present her husband with a son or daughter. I persuaded Arthur to stay an extra day so we could saddle two horses and gallop about the countryside. By the time Arthur returned to Boston, Perdita with the aid of servants, had delivered a little girl. They named her Catherine. But the joy of being a mother was brief. Perdita died three days later. A short time after the funeral Arthur accepted a business offer in England.

*(*MRS. WINGRAVE *sitting in her chair becomes animated)*

MRS. WINGRAVE

(To ROSALIND*)*

While Arthur is in London, I insist upon taking care of the baby. Mark my word, Arthur will finish the business transaction quickly and come back. He'll be lonesome for little Catherine.

ROSALIND

Mama was right. Arthur did return a few months later. He sent a coach and a housekeeper for Catherine to return to him in Boston. Mama was terrified that something terrible would happen to the child during the journey, so I offered to accompany them. I promised to return the next day. It was a week later before I did.

*(*MRS. WINGRAVE *rises.* ROSALIND *crosses to her)*

ROSALIND

(Brightly)
Mama! I'm back.

MRS. WINGRAVE

(Crosses to her, gravely)
So you finally decided to return home.

ROSALIND

(Smiling)
Must you look so solemn, Mama. I wrote in my letter that I would stay a few days.

MRS. WINGRAVE

You stayed a week in that man's house.

ROSALIND

My, my, Mama. That sounds like an accusation. A housekeeper and two servants were there also.

MRS. WINGRAVE

You promised to return last Wednesday.

ROSALIND

I tried to, Mama, but Arthur wouldn't hear of it. Catherine has become very fond of me. Every time I would leave a room she'd cry.

MRS. WINGRAVE

Indeed. Really, Rosalind, your behavior is not a bit becoming.

ROSALIND

Please, Mama. I didn't return to hear a lecture.

MRS. WINGRAVE

You can imagine what our friends are saying about your visit with your brother-in-law.

ROSALIND

Choice bits of gossip, I'm sure.

MRS. WINGRAVE

(She walks away a few steps)
A mother knows so little about her own daughter until —
(She glances out the window)
Oh. There's a carriage outside.

ROSALIND

(Smiles smugly)

I know. It's for me. I just came back to select more clothes.
                    MRS. WINGRAVE
(Astonished)
You mean—you're going back to Arthur's house?
                    ROSALIND
Yes, Mama. Arthur insists that I return. He's so concerned
about Catherine. She might have convulsions or become
deathly ill if I'm not there.
                    MRS. WINGRAVE
Indeed. I'm sure that in time she could become accustomed to
your absence.
                    ROSALIND
Perhaps so. But Arthur wants to take every precaution. And
now I must run along and pack.
(She turns away)
                    MRS. WINGRAVE
Tell me, Rosalind—are you doing all this just for the affection
of little Catherine?
                    ROSALIND
(A pretense of innocence)
Why, Mama. What are you implying.

(ROSALIND crosses down right as MRS. WINGRAVE exits off left)
                    ROSALIND
Living in Arthur's house was the proper setting for me to prac-
tise my insidious arts. Dressed in a becoming gown I would
busy myself over a piece of tapestry while my little niece played
about on the carpet. I would call her affectionate names and
amuse her. All of this was done for Arthur to observe.
(She crosses to center)
During those long winter evenings I was propriety itself. I
would light a candle, make a most respectful curtsy before
him, and march off to bed. How long would Arthur remain
silent before declaring his intentions—I kept asking myself.
Within a few weeks he became a pressing suitor and I accepted
with proper decorum.

(She crosses to table and picks up the wedding veil)
Our wedding was a private celebration. Malicious gossip said it was done with secrecy so the late Mrs. Lloyd wouldn't hear of it.
(She replaces veil on table)
To all appearances our marriage was a happy one.
(She crosses down)
There were, however, two blots that spoiled its perfection. During three years of marriage I had failed to give Arthur a child. And the other blemish — Arthur had suffered heavy losses of money.
(She crosses toward center)
Despite these failings I tried in a limited way, to conduct myself like a woman of fashion. For a long while, however, I was possessed by a nagging thought. I spoke about this to Arthur one evening.

(ARTHUR enters from down right and crosses toward her)
ARTHUR
That was a delicious dinner, dear. If you'll excuse me, I have some papers to look over.
(He crosses left a few steps)
ROSALIND
Before you go to the study, Arthur, I'd like to mention something.
ARTHUR
Very well.
ROSALIND
Sit down a minute, will you, dear? It's rather difficult to explain.
ARTHUR
(He sits on chair)
What is it, Rosalind?
ROSALIND
(Paces)
You must admit, dear, that I never complained when our

mode of living became more thrifty. We had to dismiss a servant — we can only afford a few social events — and I never dare
buy a new dress.

ARTHUR

I agree. And you accepted it most graciously.

ROSALIND

(After a slight pause)
Then isn't it a pity to have all of Perdita's lovely jewels and fine
clothes locked in a trunk?

ARTHUR

There's a reason for that. Catherine is to wear them — when
she's old enough.

ROSALIND

Oh. Well, that's a lovely sentiment, dear. But Catherine is just
a child. All those gorgeous silks and satins will be wasting
away. And the style then will be completely different. I — I
thought it might please you if I would wear them.

ARTHUR

(Firmly)
Sorry, Rosalind. That's out of the question.

ROSALIND

But why, dear? To keep them locked up in the attic for another
twenty years seems absurd.

ARTHUR

(He rises)
I cannot permit it. It's a promise. An oath.

ROSALIND

An oath? To whom?

ARTHUR

To Perdita. It was her wish — the evening she died — and I promised.

ROSALIND

(Hotly)
And pray, what right had Perdita to dispose of my future? And
what did she leave for me? Nothing!

ARTHUR

Please, Rosalind.

ROSALIND

I could always wear clothes better than she. Wouldn't you say
so, Arthur?

ARTHUR

Yes, I suppose so.

ROSALIND

Then shouldn't I be welcome to what my sister left?

ARTHUR

I'm sorry, Rosalind. I cannot break my promise.
(He puts his arms about her)
Try to understand, dear.

(ROSALIND breaks away from his embrace. ARTHUR *crosses up
a few steps, his back toward audience)*

ROSALIND

(To audience)
A few days passed before I mentioned the subject again. When
I did, it resulted in another quarrel. Then Arthur crossed to
the desk and took a key from a drawer. It would unlock the
trunk.

ARTHUR

*(He turns and crosses to her. Angrily, he throws a key to the
floor)*
There's the key. It's yours—and may God forgive me.

ROSALIND

(Crossly)
Since you're so angry about it, put it back.

ARTHUR

(Sharply)
You will nag until you have your way. So go ahead. Flaunt
yourself in her gowns and jewels. Little you care that you're
depriving my daughter of what is rightfully hers.

ROSALIND

Go on. Call me vain, callous, selfish.

ARTHUR

Those names fit you well.

(He paces away a few steps)
Do you think you'll enjoy wearing your sister's finery?
ROSALIND
What an absurd question.
ARTHUR
Knowing that you deliberately refused her last wish.
(He crosses upstage, his back toward audience)
ROSALIND
(Crossed down right)
The next evening when Arthur came home from business, I
was nowhere in sight.

(ARTHUR turns and crosses left a few steps)
ARTHUR
Rosalind. Are you upstairs?
(He hurries off up left)
ROSALIND
In vain Arthur searched every room for me. He called my
name as he went up to the attic.
ARTHUR
(Off, anxiously)
Rosalind! Please answer. Rosalind! Oh, there you are. Why—
(Then he utters an audible gasp of horror)
ROSALIND
Why did Arthur gasp with fright? My body was on the floor,
lifeless, in front of the unlocked trunk. Gowns of satin and
velvet were beside me. But there was an expression of terror on
my face. On my neck were ten hideous wounds made by two
vengeful, ghostly hands. Perdita had her final revenge after
all. And this is my punishment. My soul cannot rest. I must
relive my wrongdoing over and over.
(She exits slowly off right)

Curtain

PRODUCTION NOTES

Properties:
  On small table — Wedding veil.
                   String of pearls.
  ARTHUR — A key.

Costumes:
  ROSALIND, PERDITA, and MRS. WINGRAVE are ladies of elegance, so they wear tight bodices with full skirts of rich material.
  BERNARD and ARTHUR wear tight trousers, frock coats with waistcoats. A white or black silk band is wrapped about neck. They wear side whiskers.

The Decoy

An updated treatment of a supernatural tale by Algernon Blackwood.

CAST OF CHARACTERS

JOHN BURLEY — A robust, middle-aged business man
NANCY BURLEY — His provocative young wife
CAPTAIN HARRY MORTIMER — An ardent young male

Setting — In front and inside an empty country mansion.
Scene 1. An evening in June at sundown.
Scene 2. Next morning about 2 a.m.

The Decoy

The down right area represents the lawn. A door to the mansion is up right. A room inside occupies most of the acting area. A large window downstage faces the audience. The room is bare except for a scuffed armchair and an empty crate up center. Another door is at left.

JOHN BURLEY, carrying two folding chairs and a lantern, enters from down right. After giving a satisfied glance at the house, he turns and calls to those following him.

JOHN

Come along, you two. You can explore the place later. Let's get this stuff in the house.

(NANCY, carrying a sweater, a pillow, magazine, book, and thermos bottle, appears)
NANCY
A few of these goodies should help pass the time.

(HARRY carries in a hamper and a bottle of wine)
HARRY
(Brightly)
Friends — food — wine — just like going on a picnic.
NANCY
Ghost hunting is more like it.
JOHN
(Proudly indicates the house)
There it is — and all mine. In six months it'll be operating as the Pine Hill Convalescent Home.
HARRY
That'll be a change from what they used to call it — the Hangmen's House.
JOHN
So I heard. But I had to ignore those rumors. I am only concerned about what is real. Everything here from the car?
NANCY
Yes, dear. I brought along something to read — and playing cards — should we get bored with the long wait.
(Looking front)
That's a poor excuse for a flower garden out there.
JOHN
Oh, I forgot the flashlight in the car.
HARRY
(Puts down articles)
I'll get it, John.

(JOHN *moves to doorway and enters the room. He puts down lantern, opens the folding chairs and places them up center. The above happens during the following dialogue*)

HARRY
(Fondly, as he places arm around NANCY*)*
Darling, it's wonderful being so close to you again.

NANCY
(Responding)
Marvelous. And we could do this more often but your ship is always sailing away.

HARRY
You look delicious.
(He presses close for a kiss)

NANCY
(Breaking away)
Harry, we must be careful. Remember, John invited you here — after I convinced him that three was a better number for this skullduggery.

HARRY
It was easy talking me into it.

NANCY
Go on, sweetie. You promised to get the flashlight.

HARRY
(Giving her a squeeze)
I'll be back for more.
(He dashes off)

(JOHN *opens door and calls*)
JOHN
Come in. The sun has gone down. Let's carry this out as we planned.

(NANCY *crosses to doorway as* HARRY *returns with flashlight. He picks up hamper and bottle and follows* NANCY. JOHN *is lighting the lantern as they enter the room*)

                    JOHN

The electricity isn't turned on yet. So this must do.

                    HARRY

The house smells like an empty museum.

                    NANCY

(With humor)

Perhaps bodies are buried in the floor.

(The various articles are placed about the room)

                    NANCY

(Pointing left)

What room is out there?

                    JOHN

That was the library.

                    NANCY

Ah, yes. Where it all happened.

                    JOHN

Place your chairs around as you like.

(Indicates the scuffed armchair)

I'll take this one.

(He shoves empty crate toward NANCY'S *chair)*

Here's something for your feet, Nancy.

                    NANCY

(Sits)

Thanks. Not exactly the comforts of home.

                    JOHN

(Genially)

Of course not. So we tolerate a little discomfort. And if you
remember, Nancy, it was your idea to have this night watch.

                    HARRY

(Sits right of NANCY*)*

John, you didn't tell all when you invited me. I know this house
is supposed to be haunted — and we're to stay here until morning. But why?

JOHN

Let Nancy tell you. She knows the history of the place.

NANCY

Not exactly. But as it was told to me, the house was built about fifty years ago. A Mr. Thompson became the first owner. He committed suicide by hanging there in the library. After that, whoever owned the house did the same thing. They say an image of a man appears to the one who is to die.

HARRY

Keep going. It sounds like a Hitchcock thriller.

JOHN

I don't go along with that. Only cowards or lunatics kill themselves and I'm neither one.

HARRY

But I'm still in the dark. Why are we here when—

JOHN

(Interrupts with heavy humor)
So one of us can die.

NANCY

Please, John. Don't be dismal. While you were away on a cruise, Harry, the newspaper played up the whole story.

JOHN

Since I just bought this place, that kind of publicity I don't need.

HARRY

You say a figure appears. Is it a ghost?

NANCY

It's supposed to resemble a man—and he changes.

JOHN

How changes? Clothes, you mean, or what?

NANCY

No, dear. According to the story he shows himself each time to the man who—

HARRY

The man who?

NANCY

He appears to the man who dies—as himself.

HARRY

Oh. Like a decoy. That's a new twist. Each time the man sees his own double—before he hangs himself.

JOHN

So we're spending the night here to stop all that nonsense. Tomorrow I'll make it my business to tell a newspaper reporter that we proved all those rumors were hogwash.

NANCY

Let's say, the spell will be broken.

JOHN

(Crosses to window)
And the home will get off to a good start. Before long all sorts of flowers will be blooming out there. The entrance to the house will be changed—and all sorts of improvements, of course. I like to think that inside these walls lives will be saved.

(HARRY reaches over for NANCY'S hand and presses it fondly during the above speech)

(Sound—A thud is heard off stage left)

NANCY

What was that noise?

JOHN

The wind, probably. Doors and windows are left open to let the paint dry. I'll go and see.
(He picks up flashlight and goes off at left)

HARRY

(Urgently, as he leans toward her)
Nancy, can't you see? You're wasted on him. He never thinks of you as a woman. You're a child to him.

NANCY

(Rises and moves away)
Please, Harry. This is no time for rash opinions.

HARRY

You said so yourself, he doesn't love you. His whole life is wrapped up in putting over business deals—like this house—making money to invest in another deal. As a wife you're only a convenience to him.

NANCY

Why are you telling me this now?

HARRY

Because I want you to leave him. We spoke of this before and you promised to think it over. We can arrange to—

NANCY

(Interrupts, as she hears footsteps)
Sh!

(JOHN returns)

JOHN

Nothing mysterious around in there. Hey, how about a sandwich and a cup of coffee?

HARRY

Make that for two.

NANCY

(With a brief salute)
Aye, aye, captain. But let's save a sandwich for that ghost—should he be flapping around.

JOHN

Go on, Nancy. Have your little joke.

(Curtain is closed or lights dim for a few moments to denote the passing of five hours. For a classroom production, a member can step front and announce, "The time is five hours later")

(When curtain or lights come up, NANCY is seated on chair asleep. Her head is resting on a pillow, sweater over her shoulders, and feet propped on crate. An open book is on her lap. HARRY, seated at her right, is playing solitaire on the

hamper in front of him with a pack of cards. JOHN, *seated at left, is busy writing notations on a pad)*

NANCY

(Stirs and wakes up)

Where—where am I? Oh.

(Tosses book on floor)

This book is a murder mystery but it put me to sleep. What time is it?

JOHN

(Glancing at watch)

Almost two o'clock.

NANCY

(Rubs her hands and buttons up sweater)

Ooh. It's getting cold in here. Did I miss anything?

HARRY

Sure. A skeleton came in and did a tap dance.

(He reaches for wine bottle beside him and pours a drink)

Anyone joining me?

NANCY

Why not? Let's pretend this is a party in a fun house.

(She accepts drink)

JOHN

(Looking up from pad)

I've been figuring out a work plan. Now if the electrician starts next week, then by—

(Sound—Another thud is heard from off left)

NANCY

There's that strange sound again.

HARRY

Perhaps the skeleton is practising up a new routine.

JOHN

(About to rise, to NANCY)

If it bothers you, I can—

NANCY

(Interrupts, as she rises)

No, let me. Please. I'm curious. I haven't been out of this room since we came.

JOHN

You really want to?

(NANCY nods)

Okay. We're right here if you need us.

NANCY

(Moving to left)

I'm not afraid of things that go bump in the night.

(HARRY rises and follows her with flashlight)

HARRY

It's dark out there. Take this along.

(NANCY takes flashlight and leaves. HARRY, at doorway, looks after her)

JOHN

Don't look so concerned, Harry. She's all right. I know her better than you do. Close the door.

HARRY

But Nancy may call and —

JOHN

(Interrupts forcefully)

I want a word with you. Shut the door.

(HARRY does so)

Come here.

(HARRY moves closer)

Let me warn you. If I thought you two were lovers — if it is anything like that — then one of us should remain in this house — a dead man.

HARRY

(Covering up his guilt)

John, you're talking wild. We're old friends. How can you think —

JOHN
(Breaks in)
I trust Nancy completely. Understand? If I lost that, I'd lose
my faith in women—my desire to live.

HARRY
(After a pause, tries to be casual)
Come now, John. You shouldn't brood over something
that—that never happened.

JOHN
Always ready with a glib answer, aren't you? It won't do this
time.

(NANCY returns from the library)

NANCY
(Assumed cheerfulness)
Boys, the mystery is solved by Nancy Sherlock. There's a bell
rope out there and it's hitting against a metal sheet.
(A more serious tone)
How much longer do we play this game of hide and seek?

JOHN
I'm sorry if it's getting tiresome. We agreed to leave as soon as
it gets daylight. Remember?
(Rises and takes flashlight from NANCY)
Funny, I don't recall seeing a bell rope out there. I'll have a
look.
(He crosses toward left door)
Back in a few minutes.
(He exits)

(HARRY, agitated, paces about)

NANCY
How about you, Harry? Aren't you curious to see what's out
there?
(Notices his distressed look)
What's the matter, sweetie?

HARRY
(Excitedly)
We were all wrong about the old boy not knowing. He does.
NANCY
Knows what?
HARRY
About us. Just now he warned me. If it was like that between
us—then he or me—should stay in this house—a dead man.
NANCY
I—I can't believe that John would say—
HARRY
(Interrupts)
Because he loves you—that's why he said it. Don't you see?
He'll kill me!
(Nervously paces about)
What is this—some sort of trap? Perhaps for some crazy reason
you and John want me to die.
NANCY
Don't be absurd. Why would I make excuses to John so that I
could see you, if I didn't care?
HARRY
Perhaps you were only pretending—and like a damn fool I
trusted you.
(He crosses toward right door)
Oh, what the hell. I'm getting out of here.
NANCY
(Taunting)
That's like deserting your ship, Captain.
HARRY
Call it what you like! It's over between us.
NANCY
All of a sudden it's different, isn't it—the way we see each
other. You're afraid and running out. I must say, John is
holding up much better than you.

(Before HARRY *can reach the door,* JOHN, *with a stern, fixed*

expression on his face, enters from the library)

JOHN

(Dull, without emotion)
I'm going out on the lawn for a moment.
(He walks stiffly through doorway and exits down right)

(NANCY and HARRY stare at JOHN as he moves along)

NANCY

(After a pause, alarmed)
Harry, you saw? You noticed?

HARRY

Yes.

NANCY

He — he was different. The eyes — that strange expression — the
way he spoke. That wasn't John at all.
(She rushes to window. HARRY follows)

HARRY

(Looking down right)
There he goes. He's walking away.

NANCY

(Frightened)
Oh. Don't you see? That was — the image. Remember? It takes
on the likeness. It came in here to deceive us — to give John
time to do it.

HARRY

Come now. How can you believe that silly rumor?

NANCY

Come along, Harry. We must go in there.
(They cross to left)
Hurry!

(HARRY hurries into the library as NANCY stands at doorway)

HARRY

(Off)
Oh, my God! Don't look, Nancy. He —

NANCY
(Breaks in)
There he is. He did it. He hung himself with that bell rope.
(She sobs and collapses on chair as HARRY *returns from the library)*

Curtain

PRODUCTION NOTES

Properties:
  JOHN — Two folding chairs, lantern, matches, pencil, pad.
  NANCY — Pillow, magazine, book, thermos bottle.
  HARRY — Hamper, bottle of wine, flashlight, playing cards,
      two wine glasses.

Costumes:
  JOHN — Conservative slacks, sport shirt, jacket.
  NANCY — Bright slacks, blouse, sweater.
  HARRY — Colorful slacks, shirt, jacket.

Sound: Thud off stage left as indicated.

The Wind In The Rosebush

A dramatic version of the short story by Mary Wilkins Freeman.

CAST OF CHARACTERS

REBECCA FLINT — A tall, resolute woman of middle age
EMELINE DENT — A plump, blonde woman with wary eyes

Scene — Right area of stage suggests a yard and front of house
in Massachusetts.
Center area is the sitting room.
Left portion is a small bedroom.

Time — A span of several autumn days early in the century.

The Wind In The Rosebush

On the writing table down right is a journal, a pen, ink-stand, letter, and Rebecca's bonnet. Her cape is hanging on chair behind her.

A rosebush with one red rose on it is at right in the yard area. An invisible door is up right, and a window to be imagined is along right wall of house. At center is a tea table with a long,

*fancy cover over it. At each side of table is a brightly
upholstered chair. Up center is a clothestree. Down left of this
grouping is a small desk with a chair behind it. A bedroom
type of chair is placed in the smaller area at left.*

REBECCA FLINT, *dressed in a long, plain dress of the period,
sits facing front at writing table. She carries herself erect which
gives her an indomitable appearance. For a moment she writes
in the journal.*

REBECCA
(Finished writing, she reads from the book)
For over twenty years I pursued the habit of writing about my
day in this journal. I am now weary of it. But I wish to record
here what happened on a recent journey. What occurred could
be called ghostly.
(She puts down book and addresses the audience)
Perhaps I should explain that I was a schoolteacher since the
age of twenty in a small town in Michigan. As my mother, a
widow, was always sickly and depended upon me; I remained a
spinster. She departed from this life some time ago. When my
Uncle Horace died last year, he left some property and money
to me. With this windfall I was able to give up my teaching
post. It was while I was visiting my Cousin Beatrice nearby,
that I decided to go to Ford Village in Massachusetts.
*(She continues speaking as she rises, puts on her cape and bon-
net)*
My sister, Grace, had lived there with her husband, John Dent,
and their daughter, Agnes. After my sister died — almost five
years ago, he married again. A short time after that I was in-
formed that John had also died. It was lonely living alone, so I
decided to bring Agnes, my niece, back with me.
(She crosses to right of table and picks up piece of baggage)
A long train ride and a ferry brought me there. A boy in a
wagon drove me to the home of my brother-in-law. In a few
minutes I was to meet for the first time, his widow, Emeline.

*(EMELINE, dressed in silk finery, enters from up left and crosses
to door)*

REBECCA

(Crosses up)
As I walked toward the house the front door opened.

EMELINE

(Smiles placidly as she extends her hand)
You are Miss Flint, I suppose.

REBECCA

Yes. I am Rebecca Flint.

EMELINE

Your letter arrived only this morning.

REBECCA

Did it? I couldn't wait to hear from you, so I came on.
(Looks about)
It's beautiful here. Your lawn is trimmed smooth as velvet.
(She notices that the rose on the bush is quivering)
What a lovely rose. But why does it tremble like that—when
there isn't any wind?

EMELINE

(Startled for a moment)
Never mind. Just don't pick it.
(Then more affable)
Come into the house.

(They cross toward center. REBECCA *looks about the room)*

REBECCA

My. You have elegant furniture. Everything looks so new.

EMELINE

I was never one to use dead folks' things. Let me take your
wrap.

REBECCA

(Taking off cape and bonnet)
I suppose you saved something of her mother's for Agnes. She
will want that when she grows up.

EMELINE

(After a slight pause as she crosses to clothestree)
Yes. A—a few things are up in the garret.
(She indicates right chair by table)
Sit down, Rebecca. I was just about to have some tea and
cookies.
*(REBECCA sits right at table and EMELINE sits at left and pours
tea into two cups)*

REBECCA

*As I mentioned in my letter, I had to come for Agnes. Since
some money came to me from my uncle, I am able to bring her
up nicely.*
(She accepts tea cup)
I hope you are willing. You know, she's my own blood—and is
no relation to you—although I'm sure you became fond of her.

EMELINE

(Picks up tea cup)
Yes, of course.

REBECCA

(After a sip)
I know from her picture what a sweet girl she must be. John
always said she looked like her own mother. And my sister was
a beautiful woman.
(Puts down cup)
But I want to see for myself. Where is Agnes?

EMELINE

(After a slight pause)
Oh, she went to a neighbor's house for a little visit.

REBECCA

Isn't it time for her to be coming home soon?

EMELINE

Most any time now. But when she goes to see Addie Slocum,
she never knows when to come home.

REBECCA

(Picks up tea cup)

If Addie is such a good friend, we must have her come out to see Agnes when she's living with me. I suppose she will be homesick at first.

EMELINE

Most likely.

REBECCA

(After another sip of tea)
Does she call you Mother?

EMELINE

No. She calls me Aunt Emeline.
(Breaking a cookie in two)
When did you say you were going home?

REBECCA

In a few days. That should give Agnes enough time to get ready.

EMELINE

(Bluntly)
Oh, as far as that goes, it wouldn't matter about her being ready. You could go home tomorrow, if you like, and Agnes could come afterward.

REBECCA

Alone?

EMELINE

Why not. She's a big girl for her twelve years.

REBECCA

(Puts down cup and saucer with determination)
My niece will go home when I do. If I cannot stay here in the house that used to be my sister's, I will stay elsewhere.

EMELINE

(Forced cordiality)
Now, now, Rebecca. Of course you are welcome here.

REBECCA

(Glances right at window)
There she is!

EMELINE

(Startled)

What?

REBECCA

(Rises and glances toward door eagerly)
I saw her pass the window.
(After a pause)
Why doesn't she come in?

EMELINE

I guess she stopped to take off her hat.

REBECCA

It can't take her all this time to take off her hat.

EMELINE

(Rises)
I will see.
(She crosses to door and opens it)
Agnes!
(Turns)
She ain't there.

REBECCA

But I saw her pass the window.

EMELINE

(Returns to table)
You must have been mistaken.

REBECCA

I know I did. I saw first a shadow go over the ceiling — then I
saw her in the glass there.
(She points right)
And then the shadow passed the window.

EMELINE

How — how did she look in the glass?

REBECCA

Pretty, with light hair tossing over her forehead. Was that like
Agnes?

EMELINE

Like enough.
(Turns away)

But of course you didn't see her. You've been thinking so much about her that you thought you did. Anyhow, it's too early for her to get home from Addie Slocum's.

(REBECCA *steps down and walks left.* EMELINE *reaches below table and puts bowl and spoon on it*)

REBECCA

(To audience)
I had resolved not to retire until Agnes returned. But the long trip made me weary. So I went to bed early in the evening. The next morning I came downstairs and found Emeline busy preparing breakfast.

(*As* REBECCA *crosses to center* EMELINE *is standing behind table mixing something in a bowl*)

REBECCA

Good morning, Emeline. Where is Agnes? Doesn't she help you with breakfast?

EMELINE

Not usually.

REBECCA

What time did she get home last night?

EMELINE

(Busy stirring with spoon)
She didn't get home.

REBECCA

What?

EMELINE

She stayed with Addie. She often does.

REBECCA

(Anxiously)
When will she be home?

EMELINE

Oh, I guess she'll be along pretty soon.

(Turns to REBECCA*)*

Until breakfast is ready, why don't you go outside. There's a real pretty view over the river.

REBECCA

(Deflated)

Very well.

(She crosses out the door and walks toward the rosebush. She gasps as the bush sways and hurries back into the room)

That rosebush! It's blowing!

EMELINE

What of it?

REBECCA

There isn't a mite of wind this morning.

EMELINE

(Annoyed, as she puts bowl on table)

Lan' sakes. I cannot spend my time over such nonsense. So if—

REBECCA

(Interrupts)

Oh. There she is now.

(She hurries to door and flings it open. A breeze tosses her hair)

There's nobody here.

EMELINE

I didn't hear anybody.

REBECCA

I saw somebody pass that window!

EMELINE

You were mistaken again. Please shut that door.

*(*REBECCA *shuts door.* EMELINE *arranges cups and saucers on table)*

REBECCA

(Crosses toward her, sniffing)

What smells so strong of roses in this room.

EMELINE

I don't smell anything but the nutmeg that I use in baking.

REBECCA

It is not nutmeg.

(Anxiously)

Oh, where do you suppose Agnes is?

EMELINE

Perhaps she went over to Porter's Falls. Addie has an aunt over there.

REBECCA

When would she be home?

EMELINE

Oh, not before afternoon.

(REBECCA crosses down to audience as EMELINE sits left at table. She puts bowl and spoon under it and reaches for a piece of embroidery and a white nightgown as REBECCA speaks)

REBECCA

I waited with all the patience I could muster. I kept watching the clock on the mantle until four o'clock had arrived. Then I reached a decision.

(She moves to right of table)

Emeline—I have waited as long as I'm going to. I've been here ever since yesterday—twenty-four hours—and I haven't seen Agnes. I want her sent for.

EMELINE

(Puts down embroidery)

Well, I don't blame you. It's high time she came back. I'll go right over and get her.

(She rises and walks to clothestree)

REBECCA

(Gratefully)

I wish you would, Emeline. I don't like to trouble you but—

EMELINE

(Interrupts, as she puts on shawl and bonnet)

Oh, it ain't any trouble at all. I don't blame you. You have waited long enough.
(She goes out door and exits down right)

(REBECCA sits right at table and addresses audience)
REBECCA
I sat at the window watching breathlessly for her return. About half an hour later Emeline came back — alone.

(EMELINE enters. REBECCA hurries to door)

REBECCA
Where — where is she?

EMELINE
(Forcing a laugh)
Oh, girls will be girls. She's gone with Addie to Lincoln.
(She crosses to clothestree)
Addie's got an uncle who's a conductor on the train and lives there.
(Hangs up shawl and bonnet)
He got 'em passes and they'll stay with Addie's Aunt Margaret for a few days.

REBECCA
(Dazed)
A few days?

EMELINE
Yes. Till Thursday.

REBECCA
How far is Lincoln from here?

EMELINE
(Crosses to table)
About fifty miles. It'll be a real treat for Agnes.
(She sits left at table)

REBECCA
Thursday. That will make it pretty late about my going home.

EMELINE

(Pleasantly, as she picks up embroidery)
Well, if you don't feel you can wait, I'll get her ready and send her on just as soon as I can.

REBECCA

(Firmly)
No. I'm going to wait.
(A pause while she paces nervously to window and back. EMELINE *is busy sewing)*
Is there any sewing I can do for her? It will help pass the time.

EMELINE

(Picks up garment from table)
Here. You may sew the lace on this nightgown. Agnes ought to have this before she goes.

*(*REBECCA *moves down toward left.* EMELINE *puts embroidery and nightgown beneath the table)*

REBECCA

(To audience)
I sewed feverishly until it was finished. Sometime during the night I was awakened by music floating up through the floor from the piano in the sitting room below. I ran downstairs to the room, but the piano was silent. I became hysterical and wanted to awaken Emeline, but I was able to control myself. I mentioned it to her the next morning.
(She is left of EMELINE *who is seated at table drinking from cup)*
Emeline, during the night were you awakened by music from the piano?

EMELINE

The piano? No, Rebecca. I heard nothing. You were dreaming.

REBECCA

I tell you somebody played "The Maiden's Prayer." Does Agnes play that piece?

EMELINE
A little. Sit down and have some breakfast.
(Takes another sip from cup)
REBECCA
Has Agnes come home?

EMELINE
Of course not. Have you gone crazy over that girl? The last
train came by before we went to bed.

*(*REBECCA *crosses toward left as she addresses audience)*
REBECCA
After breakfast I went up to my room for a handkerchief.
What I saw there startled me. I hurried downstairs.
(Crosses toward EMELINE*)*
Who—who's been in my room?

EMELINE
Why? What do you mean?

REBECCA
When I went up there I found that—little nightgown of
Agnes's on the bed laid out. The sleeves were folded—and
there as if holding it—was that red rose.

*(*EMELINE *appears disturbed as she slumps forward)*

REBECCA
(Concerned)
Emeline, what is it? What's the matter?
EMELINE
(Recovering)
It's nothing. I don't want to hear such nonsense.
REBECCA
It isn't nonsense. How did that nightgown get on the
bed—when I put it in my bureau drawer?
(Paces about)
Is this house haunted or what?

EMELINE

(Sharply)
I don't believe in such things. If you do, then you're crazy.

REBECCA

Not yet. But I shall be if this keeps on much longer.
(Stops pacing)
I'm going to find out where the girl is before night.

EMELINE

How?

REBECCA

I'm going to Lincoln.

EMELINE

(With a faint triumphant smile)
You can't. There ain't any afternoon train to Lincoln.

REBECCA

Then I'll go over to the Slocums and speak to them—if you'll
tell me where they live.
(She crosses down and speaks to audience)
Despite my intentions, I never went there. All afternoon and
evening there was a downpour of rain, so I couldn't venture
out.

(Moves left to bedroom area)
That evening I went up to my room and tried to read. Em-
meline was downstairs.
*(She picks up book, sits, and starts to read. She holds that posi-
tion)*

*(EMELINE crosses to doorway and picks up a letter from the
floor. She glances at envelope, then starts to move left toward
REBECCA with it. She pauses, carefully opens the envelope and
reads the letter. Possessed with a new idea, she crosses to desk,
sits and writes a brief message at the bottom of letter. It is
returned to envelope and pressed shut. She rises and crosses to
REBECCA)*

EMELINE

(Hands her the letter)
This letter for you just arrived. Mr. Amblecrom brought it.

REBECCA

Who is he?

EMELINE

The postmaster. He often brings letters that come on the last mail.

REBECCA

(Glancing at letter)
It's from my Cousin Beatrice.
(Reading some of it)
She says she misses me and has asked a friend, Mrs. Greenaway, to stay with her.
(Continues reading)
Oh. Mrs. Greenaway wrote a note at the bottom. She writes that my cousin fell down the cellar steps and broke her hip. She asks me to return at once.
(Disturbed)
Oh my. I must take the first train back tomorrow.

EMELINE

Oh, I'm dreadfully sorry.

REBECCA

(Rises, with spirit)
No, you're not. You're glad. I don't know why, but you're glad. You've wanted to get rid of me for some reason ever since I came. Now you've got your way. I hope you're satisfied.

EMELINE

Rebecca, how you talk.

REBECCA

I talk the way it is.
(Paces about)
What I want you to do is send Agnes out to me just as soon as she comes home. Don't wait for anything. You pack what clothes she's got and buy her a ticket. I'll leave the money. She

don't have to change trains. Now, remember, when she gets home you start her off on the next train.

                              EMELINE

Very well, Rebecca.

(As REBECCA *crosses toward her writing table down right* EMELINE *exits left)*

                              REBECCA

I started on my journey the next morning. When I arrived in Michigan, I found my cousin in perfect health. And as for her friend, Mrs. Greenaway, she never wrote that postscript. I realized then that Emeline had done it to hasten my departure.
(Sits behind writing table)
I wanted to return to Ford Village immediately but the fatigue and nervous strain of that week were too much for me. I couldn't move from my bed. But I could write. I wrote to the Slocums and to Emeline. When I received no reply I sent telegrams—but no response. Then I wrote to the postmaster—and finally an answer arrived.
(She picks up letter from writing table)
He was a man of few words.
(Reads from letter)
"Dear Madam. No Slocums in Ford Village. All dead. Addie ten years ago, her mother two years later, her father five. House vacant. Mrs. John Dent said to have neglected step-daughter, Agnes. Girl was sick. Medicine not given. Talk of taking action. Not enough evidence. House said to be haunted. Strange sights and sounds. Your niece, Agnes Dent, died a year ago, about this time. Yours truly, Thomas Amblecrom."
(She puts letter aside, then opens her journal and takes pen in hand)
(Speaking as she writes)
That letter brought me despair. And so with a heavy heart, I write the last sentence in my journal.

(After writing, she puts down pen, rises and slowly exits down right)

Curtain

PRODUCTION NOTES

Properties:
  On writing table—Book, pen, inkstand, Rebecca's bonnet, letter.
  Cloth travel bag by table.
  Cape for Rebecca over back of chair at writing table.
  Low pot for rosebush with red rose.
  On tea table—Long, decorative table cloth, two cups, two saucers, plate of cookies.
  Beneath tea table—Bowl with spoon, embroidery with needle and thread, white nightgown.
  On clothestree—Shawl and bonnet for Emeline.
  Letter on floor up right.
  On desk-Pen, inkstand.
  On bedroom chair—Book.

A string that extends offstage right is attached to rosebush to make it tremble.

Fan off right to blow toward Rebecca on cue when she opens door.

Costumes:
  REBECCA—Dark traveling dress of the period, cape, and bonnet.
  EMELINE—Stylish, fancy dress of a flashy color.

The Test

This is an original play by Clay Franklin written especially for this collection.

CAST OF CHARACTERS

PRISCILLA PIERCE—A small, prim messenger of gossip
MRS. BARTON—An austere widow
HESTER—Her comely, willful daughter

Scene—Inside a humble cottage in Salem, Massachusetts

Time—A late autumn afternoon around 1700.

The Test

The setting is a modest sitting room. A table is at center. Right and left of it is a chair. An armchair is down right beside a window. A stool is down left. All furniture is of plain design. Up center is a panel of wooden pegs or a clothestree. A fireplace is along the left wall. Door to outside is up right and another door up left that leads to another room in the house.

PRISCILLA PIERCE *is seated right of center table.* MRS. BAR-

TON *with a solemn expression on her face, is pacing left of table.*

MRS. BARTON
(Nervously, as she paces)
I should not listen, Priscilla. You speak infamy.
PRISCILLA
Forgive me, Martha. I bit my tongue before I spoke.
MRS. BARTON
Such shameless accusations about my daughter. As heaven is my witness, I did my best to teach her every virtue.
PRISCILLA
I know so, Martha. But alas, tongues do babble in the town. They know what friendship you bestowed upon Betsy Warren and her husband, Jonathan.
MRS. BARTON
(Sits left at table)
That we did. Jonathan was like a son I never had.
PRISCILLA
They wonder what caused Betsy's baby to shrivel and die.
MRS. BARTON
Aye. For that misfortune we did grieve.
PRISCILLA
And now Betsy is wasting away to a wisp.
MRS. BARTON
Poor child. It is from sorrow.
PRISCILLA
They whisper it is witchery—that a spell was put on the baby—and now on Betsy.
MRS. BARTON
And for that they accuse my daughter?
PRISCILLA
It is idle talk only. Like they say Hester is having sport with Jonathan.
MRS. BARTON
(She rises and crosses to fireplace)

Curse their babbling tongues.
(She thrusts the poker at the logs)

PRISCILLA

(After a pause)
I am distressed that it troubles you so, Martha.
(MRS. BARTON returns to table)
If I may be so bold, you might try her by a test.

MRS. BARTON

(Sits)
A test? Pray, what do you mean?

PRISCILLA

Heaven forgive me if it be a sin. I been reading in a book about
wondrous things. How to strip the Devil of his power — and
recite spells to bring forth good. It say in the book if one has a
curse of witchery in her, she cannot read from the Holy
Word — or even touch the book.

MRS. BARTON

You mean, that I should so test Hester — with the Bible?

PRISCILLA

Aye. Then your soul will know.
(She rises and walks to peg for shawl)
But I must tarry no longer. I made a promise to look upon
Harriet Todd. She came down with a fever. I will say a prayer
for her.

MRS. BARTON

(Moving toward her)
Priscilla, I beseech you, do not divulge what passed from our
lips.

PRISCILLA

You have my promise, Martha.
(She hurries toward door, then turns)
May you be spared from further tribulation.
(She exits up right)

(Reflecting, MRS. BARTON *crosses toward window, glances off
for a moment, then moves to table, opens the lid of a*

*decorative box and takes out a small rag doll. She carries it
with her as she walks to armchair and sits.* HESTER, *carrying a
cloth bag filled with provisions, enters from street door)*

HESTER

Mama, why do you sit in the gloom?
*(She places the bag on floor, hangs up her bonnet and cloak on
a peg)*
The market place was crowded with farmers and wagons. Such
an abundance of fruit and vegetables. I wanted to buy
everything in sight. Why are you so silent, Mama? Did you fret
because I am late?
(She lights a candle at table)
Some light will chase away those dark shadows.
(She moves to fireplace and lights another candle)
There. That is more pleasant.
(Again she notes the glum appearance)
Mama, why so melancholy?

MRS. BARTON

Priscilla Pierce was here.

HESTER

(Lightly)
Ah. Little wonder you look so distressed — with her sad tales of
miserable sinners.

MRS. BARTON

Alas, the Devil is around every corner.

HESTER

(She crosses to bag of produce and places it on table)
Fear not, Mama, I did not write my name in his black book
with my blood.
*(She picks up a small paper sack from bag and walks toward
the older woman)*
Here is a bag of sweets. Do have one, Mama. It will take away
that sour look.

MRS. BARTON

(She shakes her head, refusing the confection)

Tongues are babbling in the town about another witch.

HESTER

That surprises me not. They take delight to cast that stone.

MRS. BARTON

They say she is casting a spell on Betsy Warren.

HESTER

(She pops a sweet in her mouth)
Poor Betsy. She already walks like a dead one.
(She returns to table and places the sack in bag)

MRS. BARTON

It is also whispered that her baby died because it was bewitched.

HESTER

And I say, a blessing if it was. That shriveled, little thing! It could never have grown and become a child.

MRS. BARTON

(Severely)
That is not for us to judge. Tell me true — do you harbor any evil toward Betsy?

HESTER

No, Mama. I feel a pity for her.

MRS. BARTON

If so it be, then what is your reason for this?
(She holds up the rag doll)

HESTER

(Astonished)
Where — where did you find it?

MRS. BARTON

Beneath a bonnet in your room. I went there to mend a dress. It fell from a shelf.

HESTER

(Irritably)
Could it be you went there to pry?

MRS. BARTON

Hush! This is an evil poppet, is it not?

HESTER

No. It is a doll only.

MRS. BARTON

Mark those pins in the belly. They inflict pain when used as a spell, do they not?

HESTER

(She turns away)
Of that kind of sorcery I know nothing.

MRS. BARTON

For that, daughter, I would be thankful.

HESTER

(She picks up bag of produce)
I must put away these things. I bought a pumpkin—dried apples—some tea—

MRS. BARTON

(With authority as she rises)
Stay. I must be given proof.

HESTER

Of what, pray tell? That I—I am not a witch?

MRS. BARTON

(Nods)
I must know.

HESTER

So, you listened well to the prattle of Priscilla Pierce.

MRS. BARTON

(She opens a large book on the table)
Here. Swear a Bible oath that you did no evil to Betsy.

HESTER

(Sets down bag)
I despair, Mama, that you doubt my word.

MRS. BARTON

Come, daughter. Place your hand on the open page.
(HESTER hesitates before placing her hand on the page)

HESTER

(Quietly)

I give my solemn vow upon this Holy Book —
(She hastily withdraws her hand and turns away)
Nay, I cannot. I — I shall not be so abused.

MRS. BARTON

Alas, then it is so. The truth is not in you. They say a witch cannot look upon the Holy Word.

HESTER

I declare, you are full of strange talk today, Mama. I want no more of it.
(She tries to leave the room but a command restrains her)

MRS. BARTON

Stay.
(She indicates the stool)
Sit there.
(Reluctantly, HESTER *does so)*
Tell me. I demand the truth.
(She sits left at table)
Do you lust for Jonathan?

HESTER

Ah. More crumbs of gossip.
(After a pause, defiantly)
Since you command it, I shall be bold and speak from my heart. Had I the chance, Jonathan would be my husband. And so he declares his devotion to me — whenever we meet.

MRS. BARTON

You speak so — without shame?

HESTER

I do. Betsy was ever puny. Jonathan should have a hearty wife.

MRS. BARTON

Confess, daughter. Inside of you burns a jealousy for Betsy?

HESTER

Aye. I blush not to say so.

MRS. BARTON

Enough to do witchery?

HESTER

Perhaps.

(She darts a glance at her mother)
Your eyes accuse me. Very well. I feel no shame to tell you.
Each day as I stick a pin in the doll — I speak a verse that I
learned — and her body grows weaker.

MRS. BARTON

And where did you learn such deviltry?

HESTER

From a book of witchery that Rachel Clark showed to me.

MRS. BARTON

(She rises and crosses to HESTER*)*
For shame. That my ears should hear such wickedness from my
own flesh.

HESTER

(Rises)
I can bide my time for Jonathan. Betsy will die soon.

*(*MRS. BARTON *thrusts a stinging slap on* HESTER'S *face)*

HESTER

(After a stunned pause)
That slap does not shame me. It dares me to speak more. So
listen well, Mama.
(She strides about the room)
My desire for many a year was to wed Jonathan. By some
trickery Betsy made him marry her. It was her sin that festered
in her body and shriveled the baby. My belly will give Jonathan
hearty babies.

MRS. BARTON

(Harshly)
Fie, daughter. The whipping post is too good for you.

HESTER

So you say because I am a witch? Like those three women who
were brought to trial. I can still hear their pitiful sobs as they
were chained together, put on a wagon and sent to jail. Two
days later they marched to the scaffold where they hung by the
neck.

MRS. BARTON
(Sits on chair left of table)
I fear woe be unto you.

HESTER
I obeyed your command, Mama. Alas, truth is not always pleasing.

(Sound—A rumble of voices is heard from outside)

HESTER
Hark.
(She hurries to the window and glances off)
The road is filled with people.

MRS. BARTON
Now that I think of it, the Governor is here from Boston. There will be another trial tomorrow.

HESTER
They are shouting, "Witches. let them burn!" Do you hear?
(Hastily she walks to table, picks up doll, moves to fireplace and flings it in the flames)
There. Let it burn in the sputtering flames.
(She crosses to the seated woman. A triumphant tone).
Now let them accuse me, if they so dare. I shall deny again and again. I can recite the Lord's Prayer and the Commandments, should they so demand. No mark of the Devil will they find on my body. A witch cannot so declare. And so you will agree—will you not, Mama?

MRS. BARTON
(Subdued, she bows her head)
Let mercy be upon me.

HESTER
(With more concern)
Sit quiet, Mama. I shall bring you a cup of tea before supper.
(She picks up bag and hurries off up left)

(Sound—The voices outside come closer. They are chanting

"Witches! Witches! Let them burn!)

Curtain

PRODUCTION NOTES

Properties:
> On table—Candle in holder, matches, a book (Bible), ornate wooden box, small rag doll with several pins in it inside box.
> At fireplace—Candle on shelf, logs and poker.
> HESTER—A large burlap or cloth bag. It appears filled. small paper bag with candy in large bag.

Costumes:
> PRISCILLA PIERCE—A plain, full length, bodice dress. Bonnet. Heavy shawl on wooden peg.
> MRS. BARTON—A similar dress but material of another color. House shawl.
> HESTER—Plain blue bonnet with tie strings. Dark blue cape. Full length, bodice dress of light blue or gray color. A petticoat under dress for fullness.

Sound: Offstage voices as indicated.
Lighting: Dim until cue when Hester lights candles.